OH, SAY CAN YOU DIE?

THE ASBESTOS HOUSE OF DEATH

NON-FICTION MEMOIR

by

LAVERNE ZOCCO

ISBN: 1-4033-6682-9 (e-book)
ISBN: 1-4033-6683-7 (Paperback)

This book is printed on acid free paper.

1stBooks – rev. 11/04/02

ACKNOWLEDGEMENTS

To my two sons who lost their father and
lived through this nightmare with me.

PREFACE

This book is about a man named John who loved his government enough to die for her. Unfortunately, he did just that—not as a hero but as a victim of negligence and bureaucratic bungling.

John Louis Zocco joined the Army after the Second World War, even when he was not called upon to serve. My husband for thirty-four years, a man fiercely loyal to his Sicilian heritage, gladly served this, his beloved country, both as a soldier and in responsibilities as a civil servant. When not sporting with his sons or me, he loved to cook spaghetti sauce, play the accordion and smoke his pipe.

In the military, he was commissioned as a policeman to transport prisoners out of this country and back to a defeated Nazi Germany. John, enormously proud of his service to the United States government, was chosen to join America's Honor Guard recruited to participate in burials at Arlington National Cemetery. This squad of elite troops would fire a twenty-one-gun salute honoring presidents and enlisted men alike. He would guard doors at autopsies of fellow soldiers who died in accidents while in service for their country. He escorted bodies home to the families of his fellow soldiers and spoke kind words to the bereaved. John was the officer who folded the funeral flag and gave it to the mother of the deceased. To sensitivity and compassion, he was no stranger.

He possessed thick, wavy, dark brown hair, gorgeous, sensual brown eyes, and a smile at once inviting and beguiling. To our sons, Sam and John Junior, and to a dog named "Cinnamon," John was a hero.

As a people person and a peacemaker, John made friends easily, could talk to anyone on any subject, and would never allow a guest in our house to leave without bestowing Sicilian hospitality. Though he worked the nightshift at a local Post Office, many times he gave up his days to help friends when he should have been sleeping. He would run over to their houses to help them move, rush out to rescue someone in trouble, or hurry off to sit with a friend who needed someone to listen.

My husband made every day a joy for his sons and me. As a Godly man, he took seriously his responsibility to his Creator. His deepest peace came on Sunday morning when he sat after services in an empty church feeling God close.

John and I had many plans for our retirement. He would finish his time at the

Post Office, take his pension and relax for the first time in his life.

Those plans are now a ghost story: John is the ghost. That sentiment holds a deeply sad and dark message because death is final and incontrovertible. That is both the truth of it, and the agony of its certainty. John is dead. He will never come back to earth again. I am left with only memories.

Why couldn't my husband realize his simple plans? Why was he cut down in the prime of life? Why were our sons and I robbed of a lover and a provider? Why were his friends cheated by this tragedy?

You might ask if John was killed in an accident, or by a robber? Did he die of natural causes? The answer will surprise you.

No, John was killed by the government of the United States, the government he loved and served with honor. He has no medal to remember his heroic deeds as a citizen in civil service.

John was killed not only by his government but also by a whole host of people who were connected with his death. In one- way-or-another, they all contributed to the crime. I would not believe it if I had not lived through it. I tell you it would take an intentional act of the devil to repeat this crime, it was that incredible.

John's ghost will remain in this book. It is a tribute to him as an irreplaceable human being. I need to tell the story of how he was killed, the cover-up that followed, and why he never had his day in court.

If you pick up this book and get a warm feeling, that is John drawing you to him. Come closer and he will fill you with the truth. Perhaps then he can find his rest at last.

CHAPTER ONE
THE VICTIM

A howling September wind rattled the windows as John L. Zocco made his appearance into the world in the middle of his parents' bed. After his birth at home in 1929, in Cleveland, Ohio, his exhausted forty-two-year-old mother Mary, and his fifty-year-old father Sam, examined him and labeled their newborn "little flower" because "he will make our old age sweet."

Baby John couldn't have picked a worse time to be born. The stock market crash forced many tycoons to throw themselves out of windows. The country entered the "Great Depression," a situation so horrendous many would die of starvation and a large percentage of American workers would be out of their jobs. Added to this calamity, the hoopla of the roaring twenties, with its bathtub gin and gangsters murdering gangsters was coming to an end. The madcap party of prohibition was over.

The mewing baby was a Libra, the "sign of the scales," according to astrological belief—a good sign for a balanced personality and a peacemaker, if you believe such things. His cap of brown-black curls and the large, striking dark eyes that would soon turn to

1

inky black, foretold the boy would be handsome, a representative of his fierce Sicilian heritage.

With all the economic and cultural fury going on in the world, you might think the boy would grow up with a chip on his shoulder and scrap with other kids at the drop of a hat. You would be so wrong.

The bond between father and son grew as the boy grew. Rather than becoming a fighter, John cultivated a gentle soul. Rather than pick fights, he stepped in to break them up. Rather than be thoughtless and wild, he became compassionate and settled.

Family stories I learned when dating John reveal strong character traits. For instance, in the middle of our dates, at exactly eleven o'clock at night, he would tap his watch and head to the General Motors plant to pick up his father from his job on the nightshift. Only after he had deposited the tired man safe and sound at home could we go dancing or have a late supper. John continued this ritual five nights a week until his father retired.

His mother had not the gentle disposition of his father. When John saw storm clouds gathering across her face, he would not let her ventilate her anger. He would secretly untie her apron strings as she stood at the stove scolding him. They would both laugh as it dropped to the floor. She would berate him for tasting spaghetti sauce with the stirring spoon and not rinsing it before he stuck it back in the pot. Then he would grab her into a tight bear hug and nuzzle her neck, where she was so ticklish and vulnerable, she lapsed into spasms of laughter. But, he could not stop her from saying her rosary for him when he was out late. He never laughed about that.

In high school "little flower's" lifelong friends, Chuck and John, would sneak up to his room right off the back porch on the first floor of his house and crowd into his bed. When it was time to wake him up for school, his mother would stand with her hands on her ample hips and shake her head as she opened the door and found all three chums sleeping in her son's bed.

John's sister Theresa, who wore her long waist length hair in a braid around her head, adored him. If he deserved punishment for anything, no matter how insignificant, she would cry. All the neighbors worried when she carried baby John around on her hip, afraid she was going to end up with a permanent limp.

In his teens, John broke both his legs in a bicycle accident. Theresa paced the dark hallways of the hospital night after night praying he would be able to walk again.

When he finally came home sporting two heavy casts on both legs, his devoted sister Theresa slept in the twin bed next to his and tied a cord from his big toe to hers so if he turned in the middle of the night she would wake up and find out what he needed.

To his nieces, Marie and Frances, he was the beloved uncle who gave them first communion watches and taught them how to jitterbug. He would not get married unless "Re-Re," the youngest, could be flower girl, and Fran, the oldest, a bridesmaid.

Classmates at Shaw High School remember John as a snappy dresser, a class clown, and a steady friend who was exceedingly loyal. Other attributes: the best dancer, the best skater, and the biggest flirt in the whole school.

There we would sit, bundled up for a football game between his Shaw High, and my—rival schools. He would nudge me every time the loud speaker would announce, "That tackle was made by a Shaw High player." He told me he loved that player's name because it sounded like music rolling off his tongue. Years later when we met the hero of Shaw High's football team, John acted like a kid. Naturally, they became good friends.

John collected friends as some people collect dolls. A natural comedian and mimic, he was begged at weddings or any affair to tell stories. The guests would be found over in a corner somewhere crying with laughter. Eventually everyone gravitated over to get in on the good time.

When we were "young married people" many of our friends were in college at Miami University in Southern Ohio. They would come home broke and tired. John would gather them up and bring them to our house. I would make platters of ribs, and we would drink Chianti wine, (because it was cheap). We all told jokes into John's new wire recorder. They slept all over the floor of our front room. The next day as John played the tape back we would roll around the floors laughing at how hilarious we sounded. It was always funnier the second time around.

For our first Christmas together John wouldn't let me buy the tree because his friend was selling them. On Christmas Eve, he dragged into the house the poorest excuse for a pine tree I had ever seen. It had big holes in its branches: needles were falling everywhere: no matter which way we turned it the tree was lopsided. Even after stringing lights, smothering it with ornaments, and burying it with silver icicles, we couldn't hide the flaws. John could see how disappointed I was as I looked at the poor thing. He took me into his arms and whispered, "It made my friend very happy cause he wasn't selling many." In all the years since it remained our favorite tree in our memories.

The first time I <u>saw</u> John was in a photograph in which he was wearing army fatigues, sitting high atop a Patton army tank, smiling happily. The first time I ever <u>met</u> John was when he and a girl in my class decided to get married. I was sorely disappointed when she broke the news to me soon after that they had broken their engagement. I lost track of my friend after graduation when I went to work for the Telephone Company as an operator, and she went on to something else. Six months later, imagine my surprise when I picked up the phone and it was John's voice.

In this shy voice he said, "I think six months is an honorable amount of time to let pass before asking you out on a date. Would you like to go dancing?" I accepted in a heartbeat.

The wind was warm and the lake was like a mirror as we entered the pavilion at the Southwestern Ohio summer resort. Mellow tones from the new Glenn Miller Orchestra filled the ballroom, while a silver glitter ball hung from the ceiling painting the wall with streaks of sparkling light. We danced, we ate, and at the end of the meal John majestically handed the waiter a hundred-dollar bill. A long time afterward John told me he had his whole pay given to him in that one bill so he could impress me. A long time later I told him he had impressed me.

On our second date he took me to an air show in Willoughby, Ohio. The crowd roared its approval from the crowded stands. As the last plane came over its pilot sprayed the whole crowd with perfume. John got soaked. "It was worth it," he told me, "to be there with you."

John wanted twenty-one friends and family in our wedding party. He argued with the priest, but we had twenty-one in our wedding party. He wanted his best friend who was stationed with the Army in Italy, to be our best man. Impossible, so John had the marriage license sent to him in Italy for his signature as our best man. John played the accordion at our wedding, made reservations at a certain Motel because he liked the thought that the sign matched our initials, and rented a cottage on the lake named, "Charley Boy," for our honeymoon in honor of his best friend who couldn't come home.

In our first apartment, we had no hot water. Baths were undertaken in a child's pool that we emptied into the sink.

We kept hitting our heads on the dormer ceiling in the front room that was slanted at a sharp angle. John went into debt $3,000 for furniture to make me happy so I wouldn't think it was such a hardship to live there.

When our son, Sam, was born, my darling husband took all our friends out for "Big Boy's" at the local fast food restaurant. At home Sam had terrible colic for the first three months. I would wake up refreshed from a good night's sleep, and find John in the reclining chair in the front room with Sam on his chest, both sound asleep. They had been there all night so Sam's crying wouldn't disturb me.

I always knew I was going to lose this precious man early. In 1955 he was involved in a serious car accident. He was supposed to pick me up at his mother's house to take me Christmas shopping. When the hospital called I rushed to the Emergency Room praying all the way because they wouldn't tell me over the phone how badly hurt he was. A drunken driver, fresh from an office Christmas party, had hit John's car head-on after crossing the line. The drunk lost one tooth. Our doctor met me at the hospital and told me that John had no broken bones but that John's brain was "leaking." Our doctor had called in a specialist to see what could be done. He was an Oriental doctor who decided to put acid in John's IV and feed it to his brain, hoping it would seal the wound.   For two harrowing days I held John's hand while large tears rolled down his cheeks. "My body's on fire," he moaned. To our amazement the treatment worked but not before the seepage caused John to lose a good part of his short-term memory.   The extreme treatment also took away John's tolerance for bright lights and loud noises.

He joked about the accident, saying two undertakers in East Cleveland were sitting on top of the entrance to "Lakeview Cemetery" arguing over who was going to get his body. In reality it was the two policemen who reached the scene first who were arguing about who had jurisdiction. That's what John's "fuzzy" mind heard.

No matter how casually John described the accident, I saw the truth on a cold, snowy, gray day at the impound yard. The car's front end was smashed up to the windshield. Its steering column had gone through the roof. If John hadn't been thrown to the right side of the front seat the steering wheel would have impaled him. The battery dislodged from its engine mount, landing on the passenger's side of the seat so it had to have been thrown into John's lap. John survived only by the grace of God. I always shuddered when I thought about it, and prayed to God many times that John was not on borrowed time.

In 1961, we moved to Miami, Florida. John took a long time deciding what he wanted to do in the way of a job. He loved the out-of-doors and tried driving construction equipment, but it didn't pay much. I worked while he was looking around, and at that time, jobs were few. Good paying jobs were almost non-existent.

Then friends who worked for the Post Office urged John to take the Post Office examination. They brought my husband to a Christmas party in 1964 at the Biscayne Annex. John liked the idea of working for the government again. He had been in service with the Army as a military policeman. It would be his honor to show patriotism by becoming a civil servant.

Promptly after the New Year he took the examination. That was the beginning of the end, the first step in a chain of events in an incredible story.

Remember, John's ghost looks out at you from these pages. He was a wonderful common man who was cut down with an untimely death. When he died, his co-workers wanted to install a plaque in his honor in the Scheme Room where he worked. The government balked. Just think, how many of your fellow employees would want to install a plaque in remembrance of you? John took great pride in his family and in his children. He cried for days when we had to put our dog Cinnamon to sleep. He burned a candle in our bedroom, day and night, in front of our statue of the Madonna seeking her protection for our friend who was dying of lung cancer.

John's hard work earned him many letters of commendation and monetary rewards in his personnel file. He had the most accumulated sick leave in the Post Office over a twenty-three year period. His friends, his co-workers and his family will all tell you how they loved this special person.

We never get enough love on this Earth. People like John exude it like a huge fountain. Everyone can drink from the waters of good fellowship and feel refreshed around such people.

What happened to John will make you both angry and sad. It was a catastrophe that anyone can relate to.

This nice guy could be your brother, father, co-worker or son. I hope I have started to put John's image into your head, and his ghost into your heart. He would have liked meeting you as a new friend. I hope you will understand why this story had to be told.

CHAPTER TWO
HOUSE OF DEATH

I have never been back to see the Biscayne Annex Post Office, "house of death." I don't even know if it is still standing. The only way I have any idea of what it looks like is seeing it in the pictures I had to gather from local newspapers. It looks like a long, innocent, two-story building. A Miami Florida architectural and engineering company built this "house of death". The finished building fronted 280 feet of Northwest 21st Street and extended 622 feet deep to 22nd Street. It contained 202,000 square feet of floor space and was designed to support a third floor. The roof was to have a helicopter landing field, and the building was equipped with the latest devices for speedy handling of mail and parcel post. Its reinforced concrete, flat plate construction featured aluminum type window frames. Why would the government lease a building for 20 years paying almost five million dollars when they could have built six buildings for that price and owned them outright? They were only allowed to buy the building after ten years, assuring owners of a nice income for at least ten years with a big payoff at the end. Politics are ever so.

The government leased the building 20 years at an annual rental of $245,000 (4,900,000) with an option to buy after the first 10 years.

They said it would take approximately one year to build the building. That was not true. It was dedicated in February of 1953 and the workmen were still working on the building after that date. How long those workmen took to finish the building has never been verified, but I can tell you, the company that installed the asbestos would have been the last to leave and could have been called back at anytime for repair work.

No one could say with certainty when workers were finally out of the building for good, or how many times they had to come back to repair or replace asbestos containing tiles on the floor, on the ceiling or the walls. So says the article that was attached to the news item that was published in *The Miami News* on November 11, 1951 and February 15, 1953. This is highly important because their liability only lasted for twelve years under the Statute of Repose under the Products Liability Law.

This building was built in the administration of Dwight D. Eisenhower, President of the United States. I am not a

Democrat or Republican voter. I am an Independent, so I have no biases against the Republican or Democrat parties. Whatever comes out in the story regarding the politics of the participants is factual and not designed to damage either party's reputations.

Biscayne Annex was a boondoggle of the Republican political bosses of Florida. *The Miami Herald* photo shows the dedication of the building on February 22, 1953 and that the Postmaster General was a Republican cabinet member under Eisenhower. The others sitting on the dais were the national committee chairman from St. Augustine, the assistant postmaster general, the Miami postmaster, and the Republican State Chairman. It seems Republican muck-a-mucks were out in force to take credit for the monstrosity that day.

What were the government's contractors and its architect and engineering firms responsibilities for safety regarding this building? You would think that all three entities were equally guilty in allowing the installation of a lethal material like asbestos into the building. I say they were, along with all the small companies that helped install the asbestos. They were all guilty since asbestos, at this time, had been cited as causing lung cancer and asbestosis as early as 1926.

I first blame the installer whom I will call the big company. If this company were dealing with known lethal material, it should have done research to establish whether or not it could be used. Its number one responsibility was not to infest a public building with known cancer-causing material. It was up to them to understand that such material could endanger the public who became exposed while in that building, and to protect the employees who were innocently ignorant of the consequences of working in such an atmosphere. They did nothing.

In 1953, when John and I bought our own home in Willoughby, Ohio, it was a familiar practice even then to install asbestos insulation to keep the house warm. But, both my husband and I had read newspaper articles about the asbestos being torn out of a school building at the time. John wisely refused to have the asbestos installed in our house.

Now if a layman knew enough not to endanger his family with cancer, why didn't the people of the Engineering firm who did this for a living day in and day out?

Where was the government's leadership when it came to investigating what was going into the building? They had loads of safety inspectors, even in those days, whose responsibility was to make sure the building was safe for the public and the workers. That was the responsibility of both the state and federal inspectors. How come no one came forward to stop this installation of that murderous material into that building? Today they all say the danger of Asbestos was not known at that time, but that's pure hogwash. You will see in the following chapters why that was pure hogwash and why they were purely trying to cover their tracks because no one wanted to be accountable.

And how about the architectural and engineering company responsible both for the design of the building and for what went into it to guard against heat and cold? If one side of that firm was an engineering component, then they should have been well aware that asbestos was not the material to go with, because of its ability to cause lung cancer in workers exposed for long amounts of time. None of these three entities were ready to stop the erection of this house of death. It boils down to one thing, as all such boondoggle projects do—money—money—money. Instead of constructing the building outright, the government leased it with taxpayers' hard-earned dollars. When things are done that don't make any sense that's when money can be involved. But elected leaders were arrogant, insensitive, and uncaring.

I assume the architects only wanted to get the building finished and get their monies. They conducted no research and read no articles about the danger of asbestos. That would have caused unnecessary problems and required more time to make the building safe. And of course, the installers were not interested in safety. They made their own workers handle this lethal material without ever telling their own men that it could cause lung cancer.

And so we have a conspiracy of silence and premeditated murder by omission. I say these people murdered John. They also murdered any member of the public that was exposed to that building at the time, and later developed lung cancer.

Let's talk about asbestos.

Asbestos is the name of a group of natural occurring minerals that separate into strong, microscopic fibers that are heat-resistant, odorless, and very durable. These qualities have made asbestos extremely effective in industrial construction. Between 1900 and 1980, some 30 million tons of asbestos were used commercially in the United States. It was used most widely from the end of World War II until the early 1970s, when its use began to decline. Asbestos use in this country decreased from 240,000 metric tons in 1984 to 84,700 metric tons in 1987. But it's still being used and is still killing people.

Asbestos has been used in construction of thermal and acoustical insulation, for fireproofing, roofing and flooring felts, vinyl floor tiles, pipe insulation, cement piping, and as decoration on exposed surfaces. It also is used in friction products such as brakes, trucks and automobiles.

The potential for an asbestos-containing product to release fibers depends on several factors, including the location of the asbestos and how friable (easily crushed or pulverized) it is. Friable asbestos is likely to emit microscopic fibers when it is disturbed. The fibrous or fluffy spray-applied asbestos materials used in many buildings are generally more friable than materials such as vinyl floor tiles.

The Biscayne Annex was loaded with friable asbestos. It floated down like snow from the ceiling and from the walls. John used to come home with his black hair looking like it had a layer of talcum powder on top, and he used to shake it out of his clothes. He and his fellow workers toiled in that poisoned atmosphere since 1953 and beyond, in John's case, since 1965.

Asbestos tends to break down into a dust of tiny fibers that remains suspended in the air for long periods and can be easily inhaled. Because of their durability, these fibers can stay in the body for years. In general, asbestos-related diseases have a latency period of 20-40 years after exposure. They are currently seeing asbestos-caused diseases in some workers who were exposed to asbestos during World War II.

Lung cancer has become the most frequently occurring, asbestos-caused disease. It is more likely to occur in the exposed persons if they are smokers. We will get into that too. Mesothelioma, an incurable cancer of the chest and abdominal membranes, can also be caused by the inhalation of asbestos.

A lot of inhalation went on at the Biscayne Annex night and day—not only by the workers, but also by the general public who entered the building. So far, mesothelioma has been associated with exposure only to asbestos. Other cancers, mostly of the digestive tract, have also been attributed to asbestos exposure. Asbestos also causes Asbestosis, a chronic disease of the lungs that makes breathing progressively more difficult and can lead to death.

The Biscayne Annex is covered with red danger warning notices, trying to keep the public away. They cry out that the building is lethal, deadly, and dangerous. The federal government, the architects, and the contractors didn't give the employees that warning when the building was built in 1953.

Instead, they stood by and watched innocent employees march into the deadly interior to go to work. They didn't tell anybody until 1977 that they had exposed all the workers to a lethal substance that could cause cancer finally admitting the building was a death trap. They allowed them to work in that dangerous environment from 1953, when the doors were first opened and the building dedicated, until 1977 when they rushed everybody out of there. That is twenty-four years of exposure for every man, woman and child who entered the building, not just the employees.

They claim ignorance, but that is no excuse. Articles dating back to 1926 appeared in the literature of medical journals. Field-wide articles warned government, contractors and engineers that asbestos would cause lung cancer if exposure were long enough. In 1952 they knew it, and they ignored it. Neither the government, nor the architects, nor the contractors who installed the asbestos knew what the hell they were doing. They did not research or investigate the facts behind what they were plastering all over that building.

There is no excuse for such negligence. If you run a business and sell a product that is going to be installed in a public building, it is a moral imperative that you know everything you can about your product. If it is portrayed as lethal and carcinogenic you stop selling the product.

The federal government was liable, the architects were liable and the installers were liable. There is no saying, "We didn't know." It was their duty to know.

John L. Zocco, Sr. took the Post Office examination in August, of 1965, twelve years after the house of death had been constructed. He was nervous about going down to the Federal Building in downtown Miami where the test was being held. It wasn't that he wasn't confident he would pass he just wanted the job so badly. We talked it over the months after he put his application in for the test, but when the time came for him to take the test he was deathly afraid he was going to fail. If only he had.

My husband was notified four weeks after the test that he had passed with a top score. John was the happiest guy around. He felt bad that he would have to give up his job at

Roger's Tavern on 163rd Street in North Miami Beach, but he had talked it all over with his bosses. They understood but were sorry to lose him. They gave him a lot of encouragement when he went to take the test, as did all the denizens of the bar.

He let out a long sigh of relief when he showed me the letter that informed him he had passed the test. He talked about how things would soon get better. He would receive sick leave, vacation time, overtime, and life insurance. He would join the union first thing for job protection. He could save government bonds and, for the first time in our married life, we would have enough money to live comfortably.

He never saw any downside to working for the government. Do you think if the government, the architects and the contractors had told John, the day he applied for the test, that he would be working in a building bulging with asbestos (known to cause lung cancer) that he would have taken the job? They just never told him.

Do you think anybody would go willingly into that building if informed of such lunacy? How many were exposed? No one knows. How many developed lung cancer and didn't know from where they got it? We'll never know. Didn't the government, the architects and the contractors commit conspiracy and premeditated murder by not reading all the medical reports on asbestos? And don't you think their going ahead and putting in the asbestos anyway was a criminal and prosecutable offense?

John almost wasn't accepted as a postal worker. For the first time in his life he had developed high blood pressure and almost didn't pass the physical. He was devastated and so was I. The Post Office doctor sent him home and told him to rest overnight. The next day when he went back to be examined once again by the doctor, his blood pressure was down and he passed the physical.

Nothing stood in the way of our dreams now. On November 24, 1965 he was issued his formal papers of appointment and told to report to work the next day.

Because of his Army time, John received eighteen months of reward. His <u>official appointment date</u> became June 7, 1964, eleven and a half years from 1953 when the house of death was constructed, and six months after he had first been exposed at the Christmas party he attended in 1964. This is very important to know.

Another thing that is also important to establish is the definition of, "murder." Webster's II New Riverside University

Dictionary defines murder as, "1. To kill (a human being) unlawfully. 2. To kill brutally or inhumanely. 3. To put an end to: DESTROY. 4. To escape punishment for, or detection of, a blameworthy act." Every one of those definitions comes into play in the murder of my husband. You will see how I connect them up as we go along.

John had to serve a six-month probationary period after he was accepted for employment. That meant this poor man with half his memory gone had to memorize 1,000 cards by rote, and be able to identify the carrier's number by the addresses on the cards. That means he had to memorize 1,000 different addresses, and know the boundaries of the whole of South Florida, so he could throw those cards into the right slot for the assigned carriers. He had to know every carrier's code and district.

We spent every morning out on the porch in front of a makeshift Coca-Cola case marked with the carrier's numbers. John threw a thousand cards by memory and I timed him. For the final examination he would be expected to throw those thousand cards in six minutes with only three errors. It was amazing to me, that with some of his brain burnt by the acid my husband could remember anything. But, he did it. Six months later, after he took the test, he scored one hundred percent, and was approved as a career employee of the Post Office.

The President of the contractors, states in his deposition that the government, architects, inspectors, federal and state, and contractors approved the use of asbestos in Biscayne Annex and the asbestos used to spray Biscayne Annex was bought and shipped from mines in Canada.

CHAPTER THREE
THE SHUT DOWN

My husband went to work for the house of death when he was thirty-six years old. He died exactly twenty-two years later of lung cancer and asbestosis—right on schedule, according to the medical studies. It takes anywhere from twenty to forty years for lung cancer caused by asbestos to seize its victim.

By 1977, John had been working in the lethal building for twelve years. He had started as a mail sorter, working at the cases on the main floor. In no time he became a temporary supervisor. He delighted in wearing a tie and white shirt, happy to be off the high stool that workers sat on to case the mail. The men and women that he supervised told me they loved him. He was fair and helpful, but maintained a no-nonsense style to get the daily jobs done. He did everything with a sense of humor. Never in his entire tour as supervisor did he ever have a grievance filed against him.

During the dozen years he was trapped in that building, new mail-sorting machines arrived. They are now used in all post offices across the country. These efficient machines hold rows of unprocessed mail, each fed into a conveyor belt one letter at a time. The letter is then stopped in the center of the belt right in front of the seated operator who has one second to read the zip code and key the letter to its proper destination. To do this job, the operator had to be trained to memorize zip codes not only in Miami but throughout the country. They were tested on this knowledge by having to run 750 cards in five minutes with only three errors. When learned by rote the operation became like second nature to the operator. They got so good at it they could run the pieces of mail while wearing headphones and listening to music. The eyes were most important in this job, working in tandem with memory areas of the brain. John was transferred to the machines where he became a clerk several years after entering the postal service. Again, I was amazed at how well he could memorize even with his cranial injury. He liked working on the sorting machines and spent many years at that job.

About halfway through the years John spent at the Biscayne Annex he was again made supervisor—this time on the sorting machines. Then a position opened up in the Personnel Department in the "Scheme Room." John bid for this job and got it easily. He was a teacher, passing along the skills he had learned on the sorting machine to new employees. He instructed them both in the operation of the machine and in the memorization of the codes. Some workers did well, others were so nervous they couldn't concentrate, especially when taking the final test.

John related to me stories about each new employee, how he would help them get through the grueling process of learning. He devised a little scam. When the day came that they were ready to take the test, he told them he was going to give them a practice test just to calm them down, "just to get them used to the timing." Most of them were so relaxed during the "practice test," they passed with flying colors. And that was the score John recorded. They never knew there was no such thing as a practice test. Their gratitude was telling my husband they would always remember what a wonderful man he was.

My daughter-in-law's mother, a nurse, walks with senior clients at the mall for daily exercises. She met a friend and her husband who just happened to work at the post office at the time. She mentioned that her son-in-law's father, John, worked down there too. When she mentioned John's name, the man's face beamed. He gave her a ten-minute talk tribute on what a wonderful guy he was and how everyone "adored him."

I can never remember anyone ever giving a total stranger a ten-minute talk about how wonderful I was. Such events are rare.

John worked in the Scheme Room and had his desk in the Personnel Office. He worked next to a woman with whom he became great friends. They both worked in the same office, in the same part of the building. She was a cigarette smoker, and a lovely woman. Nearing the end of the twelve and one-half years she and John worked at the house of death she began to be short of breath, and complained of tightness in her chest. John was very concerned about her. It happened, either shortly before the twelve-year period had ended, or just a short time before, that she was operated on for lung cancer. She filed a Workmen's Compensation claim with the federal government and was turned down for compensation because she was a cigarette smoker. She had asbestos in her lungs, but she didn't know it. The federal government never had her examined to find out if it was asbestosis. She subsequently lost one of her lungs.

John was angry at the government for not paying his friend her rightful compensation. Workmen's Compensation is supposed to be a no-fault insurance. Regardless of how the disability occurred, it was to pay

29

compensation simply because this lady got sick while working for the federal government. But, they would not pay!

Imagine, the federal government not taking responsibility for their employees and denying any claim of disease that showed up while that worker worked in their building.

They were negligent for not having her examined for asbestosis or asbestos fibers in her lungs. These two illnesses were both very well documented. She should have been sent to a company doctor to determine if she had asbestosis or lung cancer with spicules of asbestos in her lungs. Instead, they blamed it on her cigarette smoking and denied her claim.

But, now the negligence continues.

Twelve and one-half years after John hung his hat in the Post Office at Biscayne Annex, and after inhaling asbestos fibers all that time, and after his friend had contracted lung cancer, THE FEDERAL GOVERNMENT CONDEMNED THE BUILDING!

That's right. The Feds put up huge red signs warning that the building was infested with asbestos. Postal authorities finally admitted that my husband's daily workplace was a death trap. They would not let employees re-enter the building. With a maudlin show of concern, officials transferred them all to the General Mail Facility by the Miami International Airport.

However, before all the employees were moved, each was x-rayed except, JOHN L. ZOCCO, SR. No notice to show up for an x-ray ever came. Both John and I were incensed. Normally cool and friendly, John sat down and wrote a letter to the Postmaster reporting that he was not scheduled for an x-ray, while everyone else in the building was.

The arrogant and uncaring post office wrote him back and told him he did not work in the most dangerous part of the building and therefore did not need to be x-rayed!

Let's make this clear. John worked with his friend. They both worked in the Personnel Office. All the employees in that office were x-rayed except John. He worked in the main part of the building, which was the most dangerous, and where all other employees worked were x-rayed. He had worked there for twelve and one half years, and they had the audacity not to x-ray him.

I urged him to write another letter, but he said it would be useless. He had gone as high as he could and that was their answer. I told him to write to his union, but he said they would be told the same thing and they would not fight it.

An x-ray might have saved John's life. The government's negligence in this matter contributed to his death. The postal employee who sent him that letter should be ashamed. I gave that letter to my attorney, after John died but I never remember him using it as evidence to show the government's negligence and liability. This would have been the first step in that process. Their denial of an x-ray had led to John's eventual death.

Right after this time John seemed to change a little. I have often wondered if he secretly went to be x-rayed and just did not tell me. If he had, he might have been told that his lungs were okay but that any really bad condition would not show up yet for another ten years. He might have been told, if he were worried, to quit the job to stop the exposure. This is all pure conjecture on my part, but I detected mild depression. My ebullient John became more quiet, more introspective and more of an observer than a participant in our relationships with friends and strangers. It was not like John. I always wondered after his death if he secretly knew something he had not told me.

After he got the letter from the post office, he put it away in a drawer and never talked about the x-ray again.

So the negligence continued. The building was condemned and all the employees were moved to new jobs at the facility by the airport. I do not remember any articles in the paper at the time about the "house of death" being an asbestos trap, but there could have been one or two. Nobody seemed to take it seriously that people could die from such exposure, not even the union. The newspapers did not do their jobs as investigators. I'm sure the government and the post office put a clamp on any publicity getting out that found them at fault. No one in the government ever owned up that the building was a deathtrap and they must have told any of their agencies, especially the Workmen's Compensation Agency, never to admit or mention to the employees who filed claims later for cancer that that building was shut down because of the lethal asbestos and how it caused cancer.

What about the dangerous world of asbestos? Paul Brodeur says it best in his book, <u>Outrageous Misconduct</u>, an indictment of the asbestos industry. Please be assured that this material has been researched and documented in author Brodeur's book. Whether I quote or paraphrase, this is all Mr. Brodeur's work. I want to credit him for his fine work.

If you opened a business to offer a product for sale you would research that product for health hazards first thing. If you found it to be lethal and dangerous, being a decent human being, you would not sell it. Not only that, but you would warn others who were thinking of selling the product of its potential for catastrophe.

The government of the United States did not do this. Installers and the architects of the Biscayne Annex did not do this, nor did the inspectors, state and federal. If they had, this is what they would have learned about asbestos. Its history might amaze you.

The dangerous biological effects of asbestos were known during Christ's lifetime. The Greek geographer Strabo, and the Roman naturalist, Pliny the Elder, saw a sickness of the lungs in slaves who weaved asbestos into cloth. That was 2,000 years ago. It was considered a wondrous mineral because it did not burn. Anything it was applied to would not burn either. It was known to be a silicate mineral. Its delicate fibers were so flexible they could be woven and worn just like cotton.

In the Dark Ages, its usage diminished greatly. Then Marco Polo, the great explorer, was introduced to it in Siberia. Huge mineral deposits in the mountains were mined. Peasants wore asbestos like woolen thread.

During the industrial revolution in the late 1800s asbestos was used extensively to insulate, line and protect from high temperatures in various processes. Soon lung disease manifested itself again.

Our modern awakening to the dangers of asbestos started in the nineteenth century when an English doctor performed an autopsy on a woman who had worked with asbestos textiles and had died of severe pulmonary fibrosis. She was the last surviving member of a team of ten men and herself who had all died of the same lung disease. The autopsy showed spicules of asbestos in the lung tissues. This established the plain connection between asbestos and lung disease. That was in 1886. Don't you think the company who installed the asbestos in the Biscayne Post Office should have known about that? But, wait there's more.

In 1858 the first autopsy in the United States was performed. The patient, ironically, was Henry Ward Johns who founded H.W. Johns Manufacturing Company—makers of asbestos textiles, roofing and insulation. It was the parent company of H.W. Johns-Manville, which claimed bankruptcy to get out of paying the thousands of lawsuits filed against it by dead and dying workers who handled their asbestos products. Scheming and bribed courts allowed them to do it, knowing they were a healthy, sound company with $2 billion in assets. Newspaper articles at that time were slanted in favor of the company. They, too, had been bought and paid for.

Mr. Johns, though, died of "dust phthisis pneumonitis," or asbestosis. Justice was served!

In France the first study of mortality among asbestos workers was completed in 1890. An asbestos-weaving mill killed fifty of its workers in the first five years of operation.

Finally in 1924 the first clear case of death due to asbestosis appeared in medical literature. The case was published in the British Medical Journal. From this point, the United States Health Department, and all asbestos manufacturers, contractors, and architects who required the lethal material to be included in their plans, were negligent in continuing to use the lethal product and to expose workers to it.

In 1917, Dr. Henry K. Pancoast, of the University of Pennsylvania School of Medicine, the country's foremost authority on pulmonary matters, observed lung scarring in the X-rays of fifteen asbestos-factory workers. In 1918 the United States

Bureau of Labor Statistics (imagine our own Labor Bureau) reported asbestos workers were experiencing early deaths and said it had become the practice of insurance companies not to issue policies to asbestos workers because of the assumed health-injurious conditions.

Finally, in 1930, the first case of asbestosis found at an autopsy in this country was reported in *Minnesota Medicine*, a medical journal. But the clear and present danger that asbestos presented as a health hazard was buried from the public by the government, along with the manufacturers, the installers and the engineer-architects with chicanery. They used stall tactics and outright deceit.

Now knowing that asbestos was a killer, those who worked with the lethal material filed claims for compensation. State legislators, working hand in hand with the manufacturers and the courts, put too many restrictions on the worker to prove injury. It has gone down as a disgrace in the Annuls of American Jurisprudence and is still going on today.

In 1932 there was such an outcry by the public for remedial legislation that Workmen's Compensation statutes for pulmonary diseases were enacted in twenty states. Why not the outright ban of the usage of asbestos?

It worked much better for employers, insurers, and politicians than it did for afflicted workers. The manufacturers were now protected against these claims by purchasing relatively low-cost insurance from the insurance companies. This provided insurance companies with new markets, and it gave politicians an easy way to assuage an outraged public. The Congress went along with harsh restrictions advocated by industry lobbyists.

Asbestos and silica dust, which are virtually indestructible, continue to react against the lungs for the lifetime of the victim.

There have been many lawsuits since 1930 and there are still thousands waiting to be settled.

So, my John, without being x-rayed, went back to work out at the airport facility; his friend did as well, minus one lung. And the negligence continued.

CHAPTER FOUR
OSHA-OCCUPATIONAL SAFETY AND HEALTH AGENCY

Where was OSHA between the time the Biscayne Annex was dedicated sometime in 1953, and in 1977-79 when the government condemned the building and moved all employees to the airport facility? It was nowhere to be seen. This was the excuse the government used when told of our lawsuit. Their representative at the Occupational Safety and Health Agency reported that since OSHA was not created until 1970, they had no role to play in John's exposure in 1964-65. Of course, that is a lie. They were up and operating in 1970, so where were they between 1970 and 1977-79 when the building was finally condemned? It took them seven years before they took any action, knowing full well that every day of that time those employees and members of the public were being exposed to killing asbestos.

This is why OSHA was created. At the time, more than 90 million Americans were working. No uniform and comprehensive provisions existed for their protection against workplace safety health hazards.

In 1970, the U.S. Congress recorded these figures:

Job related accidents accounted for more than 14,000 worker deaths. During the seven years that OSHA ignored the problems at Biscayne Annex Post Office, 98,000 people died nationwide.

Nearly 2½ million workers were disabled. In seven years that figure grew to 17 million job-related disabilities.

Ten times as many workdays were lost from job-related disabilities as from strikes.

Estimated new cases of occupational diseases totaled 300,000. By the time OSHA acted in John's case, 2,100,000 people would be affected.

Congress finally created OSHA because costs for lost production and wages, medical expenses and disability compensation became staggering. So, OSHA was not created for the workers, it was created to help the manufacturers and all companies involved in production. These were the same companies that established Workmen's Compensation in 1932 to cut their losses and give insurance companies a new huge source of revenue. In no way was the dead and dying employee ever figured into the picture other than as a nuisance and as a loss to the bottom line of net profits. Only after public outcry and union efforts was

OSHA given life. Labor unions pushed for it—not for altruistic reasons, but as a way to keep their membership happy. History shows Labor Unions and politicians have always been in bed together to get elected to the high offices of their respective institutions.

So the bipartisan Congress, knowing that both its parties would be criticized if they voted against the American worker, passed Public Law 91-596, "to assure, so far as possible, every working man and woman in the nation safe and healthful working conditions and to preserve our human resources." Did they live up to this lofty pledge? Absolutely not! What they did do was create another governmental agency with a large budget-—an agency that did nothing, at least in the case of the Biscayne Annex. Let's see what they didn't do.

Under the Act, OSHA was supposed to encourage employers and employees to reduce workplace hazards and to implement new or improve existing safety and health programs. OSHA, like every other institution in Washington, knew that asbestos was lethal. That alone was why this agency was created in the first place. Did they encourage the Post Office to reduce workplace hazards and to implement new or improve existing safety and health programs? No, they did not. If they had, they would have ordered the Post Office to condemn the Biscayne Annex in 1970, the first year OSHA was created. Nope, they waited <u>seven more years</u> while the workers and the public drew into their lungs fatal amounts of asbestos fibers—friable fibers floating in the air.

OSHA was to provide for research in occupational safety and health to develop innovative ways of dealing with occupational safety and health problems. The only thing it did was to develop a new, innovative way of allowing men and women in Miami to die by allowing the Biscayne Annex building to exist. They did no research into the dangers of asbestos or else they would have ordered any infested governmental building to be cleaned. Instead, they lied seven years later and denied the installation of asbestos in the Biscayne Annex was their responsibility because OSHA was not created until 1970 and the building was built sometime in 1953. They said nothing about the seven years they allowed the death trap to exist.

You have to remember that behind the name OSHA are office workers, field superintendents, and inspectors, etc. Just as in the Nuremberg Trials after World War II you could not find a soldier or member of the high command that was not "just following orders" when millions were killed. They all looked the other way. None of them had the moral courage to protest or object. None in high command positions wanted to take responsibility so they fled to South America. So too the workers for OSHA only their way of running was shutting down all avenues of information. Even getting information requires dealing with a morass of answering machines in the Department of Labor. When you finally do get a human voice, it belongs to a laconic and uninterested individual. And to take a case to the Workmen's Compensation Appeal Board is an adventure in incompetence by the clerks, let alone board members who never see your petition. But we will talk of that later.

OSHA was supposed to establish separate but dependent responsibilities and rights (to take pressure off Congress) for employers and employees, for the achievement of greater safety and better health conditions. Nice words, but what the hell do they mean? What is "separate but dependent?" Either OSHA was separate and independent of other governmental powers, or they were dependent upon the renewal of their budget. You can't be both at the same time. We all know that once a governmental agency is established with a budget to be spent, that the high officials kowtow to the Congress and its individual members. They are at the mercy of special-interest groups, and in this case the special interests are the manufacturers and builders of industrial complexes. That is government doublespeak you hear so often. If they had truly been separate they would have investigated the Biscayne Annex and shut it down in 1970.

OSHA was to maintain a reporting and record-keeping system to monitor job-related injuries and illnesses. John was never shown any record of his illness. He was never included in any report, other than in his death certificate. His positions, both at the Biscayne Annex, where OSHA knew the building was infested with asbestos, or at the airport facility, were never monitored. OSHA did nothing in seven years but watch John die. They helped to murder John my husband.

OSHA was supposed to establish training programs to increase the number and competence of safety and health personnel. Were they kidding? Have you ever monitored a government inspector coming into a facility to increase safety and health? John did. They would come in, stare at the ceiling, walls and floors, and as asbestos fibers dropped like snow, they drank coffee and never reported it. If they did report anything it was ignored for seven years. Government workers follow the rules and don't make waves. Not one training program put in place at Biscayne Annex increased the number and competence of safety and health personnel. And if there were, it had nothing to do with the reporting of killer asbestos in the ceiling, walls and floors, and in the breathable air.

OSHA was organized to develop mandatory job safety and health standards and to enforce them effectively. Their negligence in this one command in the Public Act created this danger to continue. They <u>saw</u> the asbestos, they <u>knew</u> of its dangers, they <u>recorded</u> the dangers, they <u>heard</u> the complaints of the workers, but they never ENFORCED THEIR STANDARDS to rid the county of a lethal death trap. They did nothing in seven years to protect the workers or the public. If they had, the workers would have been ordered to wear spacesuits and cover their faces, noses and mouths, with oxygenated helmets. They had them in 1960, so they surely had protections in 1970. That is the kind of dress they would have had to wear to protect them from asbestos in the air. The public would have been included in that order. They had already been exposed for seventeen years. What on earth would have protected them then?

Finally OSHA was to provide for the development, analysis, evaluation and approval of state occupational safety and health programs. They needed no analysis, evaluation or development. In 1970, they knew that asbestos existed at the Biscayne Annex, that it caused lung cancer, and that it was the friable type that lingered in the air for employees and the public to breathe.

The only thing they needed at the time was approval of the state. Since the state inspectors were having coffee, they were happy to give up the responsibility of murdering employees and public to the federal government, which in turn did nothing.

Up to this point it had been a state responsibility. From 1953 to 1970 when the federal government took over, the state did not tear down the Biscayne Annex. They knew asbestos was dangerous. They certainly had to have been aware of all the publicity that was being generated about its dangers. And they certainly were aware that Biscayne Annex was infested with asbestos. All they had to do was look at the state and city approved plans for the building to find it was inundated with the stuff. In our lawsuit, the state blamed the federal government, notwithstanding that it had been their inspectors that allowed the lethal material to be included in the planning and execution of the building. In doing so, they had condemned all the workers and public to lung cancer.

There is a caveat in the duties of OSHA that strives to implement its mandate fully and firmly with fairness to all concerned. Of course to OSHA, "all concerned" were the congressmen and the special interests of manufacturers and producers of asbestos.

They undoubtedly were kept from doing their job by pressures from manufacturers like Johns Manville who produced the asbestos. They must have been told if they went public with the information that asbestos was lethal, there would be panic among workers and public alike that would cause another investigation like the one in 1932 that cost the producers and insurance companies alike the annoyance of having to get around it.

They must have been told to keep their mouths shut and let the Workmen's Compensation cases be turned down by the federal government with their impossible rules for exposure. And they must have been told, if they were contacted to deny, deny, deny their responsibilities, and to allow bought-off judges to dispose of them. Why else would the state have done nothing from 1953 to 1970 when they turned the whole thing over to the federal government through OSHA? Why, too, would OSHA have done <u>nothing</u> from 1970 to 1977-79?

And now we come to OSHA's disclaimer to all the above. The Act does not cover working conditions regulated by other federal agencies under other federal statutes.

It is my understanding from what our lawyer told us that the only agency regulated by other federal agencies under other federal statutes you guessed it, IS THE UNITED STATES POST OFFICE. This means that no employee of the Postal Service, including John, could have reported that the Biscayne Annex was causing deaths from asbestos, even if they knew it as a certainty. They could not report that asbestos was falling from the ceiling, walls and in the floor, and was being breathed by the employees and public alike. They could not report that they were diagnosed with lung cancer from working in the Biscayne Annex, and that they would be turned down for Workmen's Compensation as a by-product of this ban.

Why, pray tell, would the Post Office be exempt from all the requirements put upon OSHA by the creation act? It was to eliminate responsibility of the federal government for any negligence they allowed to exist in any Post Office in the United States. It was to gag workers from speaking out as they shook the asbestos from their clothes. It was to eliminate justice through the courts by excluding OSHA from being hauled into court for its negligence. It was a way to stop lawsuits against manufacturers and architect/engineers that should have banned asbestos from being used in any public building. It was unconstitutional under the provisions for due process in the constitution, and kept the lid on the dirty little secret for seventeen years in the case of the Biscayne Annex. Even if John had realized he had lung cancer from working in the Biscayne Annex he could not have reported it publicly to the people and warn them about going into the building. It means that if he died, and his family filed a lawsuit that accused the federal government and its representative OSHA of negligence, they could hide behind this provision.

It means that congressmen, who were friends of the manufacturers or took money from the special interest group of manufacturers, would be protected by a ban of silence. It meant lawsuits would boil down to installers who claimed ignorance, and to judges who were biased in favor of the wealthy manufacturers to dispose of such claims. It allowed the Workmen's Compensation office to disallow claims from dying or dead federal workers by claiming they were all cigarette smokers, or the asbestos they showed was not the lethal kind even if it was, or their post office was not involved in the suit, or they were untimely with their claim, or a preponderance of evidence by experts in the field did not count. It allowed the Workmen's Compensation Board of Appeal to dismiss a case for lack of a material date. It allowed insurance companies to go free from responsibility by claiming that time of exposure did not fall into the state statutes promulgated by state Supreme Court justices. It was a conspiracy from beginning to end to avoid responsibility, compensation and honor. It was a way to hide murder, plain and simple.

The provision that exempted all federal employees, whose working conditions were regulated by other federal agencies under other federal statutes, means that the Post Office would have the prime responsibility of safety and health and relieved OSHA of any of its mandates when it came to Post Office employees. Since the Post Office was a department of the president's cabinet and then became a free governmental agency after that, it meant that first, it was ruled by political expediencies. After that it was cut free with its independent budget as a half-governmental and half-public enterprise.

Once again, the federal government and the congress could say that the responsibility for the safety and health of its workers was not their concern. Now the concern of an independent quasi-governmental department was unique in that its postmaster was a political appointee.

So you can see, the federal government and OSHA finally worked themselves free of any responsibility for postal employees under the creation act. Now safety and health was in the hands of a political appointee and a government agency that was not a government agency.

When any lawsuits were filed, the appellant would be hard pressed to establish negligence by anyone since the federal government said in 1953-1970 the state was responsible. And then in 1970, when OSHA was created, they exempted postal employees from the act that covered all American workers, and banned postal employees from reporting any health hazards in the myriad of public buildings used by the federal government. Then the government got rid of this albatross by cutting the Post Office department free of regulated OSHA control. It became a political entity under the power of the Congress, which furnished the money for a while and sponsored a politically appointed postmaster.

Taking it one step further, they eliminated the Congress from responsibility when they made it a self-sustaining public entity as part of the marketplace. Now all lawsuits that came down the pipe would have to go after installers who just claimed ignorance. It saved the government billions in claims by dying and dead workers, the insurance companies billions for settlements, and the compensation program billions since the judges instituted a time line that barred access to the courts.

The newly created independent post office, which even took the employees out of the Social Security Pension Plan, could claim ignorance, since they were not in existence in 1953 or 1970. They could say they were only running for a few years when the lawsuits came down the pipe after it was finally revealed that the buildings were death traps of asbestos. This was the conspiracy, which was in force when John went to work at the airport facility in 1977.

CHAPTER FIVE
THE FINAL YEAR

In the last year of John's life he experienced great changes in his behavior. He had been happy with his job throughout the final eleven years of work at the airport facility. He continued to be joyous, full of good humor and loving. Then, in 1987, he suddenly changed.

When John had urged me to go to college, I promptly enrolled. It took me eight years to get my BS while working as manager of an office. When he prodded me to go on for my Masters degree, I complained that I was too tired. But, he insisted so fiercely I finally gave in. I know now he was looking toward the time when I would have to take care of myself. He also bid on a new supervisory position in the Personnel Office that would raise his salary. In line with this change, he was enrolled in a training course based in California.

As a licensed mental health counselor who specializes in profiling personality changes, I realize now that I was seeing subtle signs that John was not his usual ebullient self. I cannot explain the cold feeling of apprehension in the form of free-floating anxiety that came over me. I couldn't put my finger on where these feelings were coming from, or why they were present. It was a constant worry that something was happening beyond my control to stop.

The first change was my husband's withdrawal from social situations. He had always been the one who took the lead in conversations with family and friends, making us laugh and giving us much pleasure. He now sat quietly with his arms crossed and became an observer. He would smile in all the right places but he would not participate in the fun. He stopped telling jokes, which was like giving up breathing for John. He appeared to be with us bodily but off in the stratosphere spiritually.

Of course we all noticed this tremendous alteration in his attitude but when we mentioned it, he would just smile and say he was a little tired, or he thought he "had a cold coming on."

In all the years John worked for the Post Office, he never once took a sick day. He had the highest sick leave accumulation that was possible to amass. The same was not true of his vacation time. Every year he took vacation time so we could visit in Cleveland with our family, or so he could stay around the house and do the big jobs of maintenance like painting. He loved to mow the lawn and putter around the yard. Sick time, though, seemed to be a matter of honor with him and had a lot to do with his self worth as a worker. He was proud of his time on the job, and had received many awards and commendations for his perfect attendance. I remember when a painful pinched-sciatic nerve in his back decked him. He would crawl around the house on his hands and knees. However, when time for work had arrived, he forced himself to dress and go. I protested loud and clear, but he said being up and walking would work the pain out of his back.

Then, suddenly John got very quiet. He gave up mowing the lawn and stopped fixing things around the house. This was also the year, when our good friend and John's former boss, was diagnosed with lung cancer. Watching her illness progress became a harrowing experience for John. Several times her husband called John to help him rush her into our hospital's Emergency Room. John always came back pale and depressed.

I also noticed my husband began attending church more often. "To pray for her," he said, but there was an air of desperation about his need to be in that quiet and sacred environment. He prevailed upon me many times to accompany him during the weekdays and just sit with him while he seemed to relax. It made him very happy.

I had learned to play the organ. Many times early in the morning, after the neighbors had gone to work, I would sit at the instrument on the porch and play a mix of lovely waltzes, contemporary songs and folksongs. After breakfast, John would go directly to bed, saying the music soothed him and put him to sleep. He never paid too much attention to what I was playing and never made any requests.

Suddenly, he started asking me to play, "Danny Boy," an especially poignant and sad Irish Air. He loved it so much I took to ending my impromptu concert with that song. One morning, when I had just finished playing, I quietly walked into our bedroom thinking I would find John sound asleep, instead I found him sobbing like a baby. I backed out into the hallway so he couldn't see me. That was the first time I definitely knew something was terribly wrong with my strong and wonderful husband.

Two more incidents led me to believe I was losing him. That year, around Thanksgiving, it was open season at the Post Office to raise employees' life insurance. John and I had talked about it that year because he had always kept the lowest amount of coverage. We discussed matter-of-factly what the cost of a long illness and funeral would mean for either one of us. When we bought our cemetery vaults from our local funeral home, I made my wishes known that it would take more insurance monies to make sure I could survive if anything happened to him. I wasn't being greedy, nor did either of us have a concrete notion that John was dying. We merely thought, innocently that it was the thing to do at that time. John was convinced he needed to raise the coverage, but he also thought it would require a thorough physical examination. I thought that wasn't true. "Open season" always meant that you could raise your insurance without an examination.

John's reaction seemed very strange. He brought home an application for the change and said he would fill it out, sign it and return it in a few days. He put the paper in a drawer of the desk in the den and never mentioned it again. He never filled it out, never signed it, and never brought it back to work. Though I asked several times about it he kept telling me he would do it, but he didn't. I think he knew he was very sick and was afraid if he applied for the raise in insurance he would have to take a physical and be turned down. If a doctor gave him a thorough examination, John feared he would find that he was very sick and make him stop work to get treatment. It is only an assumption at this point, but it makes sense. So when John died I received only the minimum insurance.

John also thought that since he was under the Post Office Pension Plan, if anything happened to him, I would receive half of his benefit, around $800.00 a month. As it turned out, after all those years of paying into Social Security and the Post Office Pension Plan, he died before he retired, so they penalized his retirement benefit. I only received $400.00 a month when he died. It was flagrant theft but there was nothing we could do about it. Imagine! After twenty-four years working for the Post Office, he didn't die when they thought he should so I was cheated out of half his benefit. But that's the federal government for you. They never told him that. Officials assured him that his family would be well covered if anything should happen to him.

John may have been frightened and in deep denial at this time. I can only imagine what beginning symptoms he was feeling from the asbestos poisoning. I'm sure he was short of breath and feeling tightness in his chest. He did show the clubbed fingers of asbestosis, but I didn't recognize that at that time, he never showed any discomfort around me, so I was totally in the dark.

The second incident happened at Thanksgiving dinner that year at our friend's house. We gathered at a long table out by the pool. John was sitting at the end of the table. Our grandson was running helter-skelter by the table, playing tag with his father. Suddenly, John lunged forward from his seat to catch him, but he kept on falling forward until his face hit the cement deck that had small pebbles embedded in it. He hit very hard and split his lip. He seemed slightly disoriented as we helped him up and was a little dizzy. He pushed us away and laughed, excusing the fall. "I just lost my balance," he insisted. Our son, Sam, seemed to notice a strangeness in the incident. "Is Dad all right?" he asked anxiously. I assured him he was fine, but in the pit of my stomach cold feelings were spreading.

Just before Christmas, that last year, I woke up early in the morning to find our bed linens soaked with perspiration. The coldness had awakened me. I was disoriented for a moment and did not understand what had caused so much water. I jumped up out of bed, now fully awake, and went over to John's side of the bed. I felt his head. He was burning up with a raging fever. His pajamas were soaked through with sweat and the bedclothes were cold, clammy and dripping wet. I woke my husband out of a sound sleep. He sat up as if he were still dreaming. I told him several times I have to change the bedclothes and his pajamas. I made him sit in a chair while I did that. He was like a child following instructions, as though he had no will of his own.

I immediately called our doctor of twenty years but his partner was on-call that night. I knew in my heart that night sweats were an indication of cancer, but I wouldn't allow the idea to take hold of me. I was in my own denial. It sat like a ton of weight on my heart. My own spirits sank. There was no way I could tell John what I feared.

The doctor told me to give John a large amount of aspirin to reduce the fever and then to come into the office the next day. Unfortunately, I had no aspirin in the house. I drove to the drugstore at 2:00 a.m. for the aspirin and bought some cough syrup as well to cut phlegm, since John was coughing a little. I came home to find him sound asleep so I had to wake him to feed him the aspirin and cough syrup.

I waited an hour and checked his temperature. Aspirin had reduced the fever dramatically; the cough medicine was working also. I allowed myself to hope it was the flu. For the rest of the night I sat by the bedside watching John as he slept.

Perhaps you can relate with my premonition of doom. I had a sinking, empty feeling in my stomach that a great trial laid before me. Tears burned my eyes. I started to think of life without John. It made me sob so hard I had to go out on the porch so I wouldn't wake him. From that point on I would have to do everything in silence, something I would do differently today.

Much is known about the stages of dying from Dr. Kubler-Ross's book, <u>On Death and Dying</u>. It was a national bestseller that was required by my college course at University. The author overlooked the stages of anticipated grief suffered by the partner who is left behind. It comes as a part of the human connection loved ones have with each other—a sort of ESP that arises subtly. Loving someone makes you privy to every one of their human responses. When responses of a loved one alter drastically over time, the other partner can feel it. The onset of grief begins long before the stricken loved one displays any physical symptoms that they are dying. A wife or husband knows when their partner is dying, even if no concrete physical evidence is available. And the grief of the one left behind begins with a horrible realization that the partner is slipping away.

Dr. Kubler-Ross listed the five stages of grief for the stricken partner as, anger, denial, bargaining, depression and acceptance. To me, the stages of anticipated grief for the partner are: disbelief, denial, playacting, witnessing, and emptiness. At first you cannot believe that anything is wrong, though your heart tells you things are not what they were. Secondly, the knowledge of coming separation creates a chilling form of denial. Thirdly, you must play act for the stricken partner, giving deep reassurance, false hope, loving support and an exterior of complete peacefulness and competency, even when your heart is breaking.

Had I had it to do all over again, I would have broken through this third restraint and talked to John openly and honestly about my feelings and fears. It would have allowed him to open up and do the same. Instead, trying to appear perfectly normal cost me the most intimate moments with my husband and stopped him from expressing his fears. We never gave each other the chance to say good-bye. We did reach out spiritually through our feelings and body language, but we never let the words fill the air.

Fourth, come the long hours of waiting and anticipating the separation and loss. All the time John was in intensive care, I didn't know if he were in pain. I jumped at every code blue called over the loudspeaker, and I cried copious tears from fear of how life would change without John. Would I be able to make it through without losing my mind?

The fifth stage of real grieving begins when you learn he has died. In that instance you are changed to a different person—a person who is truly alone. You become numb. If you are lucky you go into a kind of shock that buffers you from what is going on around you. You let the family handle the arrangements, and you allow yourself to be guided through the process by the funeral director and your personal man of God. Without faith in a higher being and a life after death, you sink into a pit of hopelessness from which some people never come out. I think what saved me from this total despair was being seen by a psychiatrist who was a friend of the family. He put me on anti-depressants immediately and forced me to work in his office where he could have daily sessions with me and keep me busy at the same time. I bless him forever and ever for his care and love.

I sat on our porch hoping against hope that death was not in our house.

The next day, John and I saw our regular doctor in whom we had tremendous faith. He related to us that there was a cloudiness surrounding John's right lung but he couldn't see much in the x-rays. He thought it was pneumonia, but he needed a lung scan to be sure. He gave John powerful antibiotics. John was scheduled to go out to California to school for his new position at work. He told me he wanted to get as high a position as he could because it would mean a big boost in pay. Silently, I think, he was telling me he was going to die but he would leave me as well off as he could.

He insisted on attending the school for a week. After taking the medication for several days he seemed greatly improved, much to my relief. The cold feeling in the pit of my stomach subsided somewhat as I watched him get into the taxi and head off for California.

During the week in California, he wrote me wonderfully loving letters filled with expressions of caring and undying passion. He lamented that he should have brought me with him. I now know he was saying good-bye.

My husband passed the test. He was now in a new managerial position, and on a new pay scale. He also seemed completely relaxed and happy, as though every worry had been lifted.

Our son Sam asked me if he could take his father for the scan. He was somewhat concerned when John almost fell down in the parking lot. But John again made light of it so Sam accepted his explanation of being "clumsy."

For the next two days, while John was at work, Sam and I sat waiting as patiently as we could for the results of the lung scan. We began praying silent prayers and thinking separate thoughts, but uppermost was always the cold fear: A great trial is coming.

It took several days for the results to be sent to our doctor. He called John and me into the office and told us softly that John had a lesion on his right lung. It was a polite way of saying he had lung cancer, not pneumonia after all. The only reaction from John was a hard squeeze on my hand.

I wanted to scream in anguish. I wanted to scream at the doctor. I wanted him to tell me what it all meant. But, I couldn't with John sitting there. Besides, I already knew what it meant. Now I slipped into the third stage—playacting.

Our doctor made arrangements for John to see a thoracic surgeon. Now added to the negligence by government, the politicians, the contractors, the architect and OSHA we were about to experience medical negligence.

CHAPTER SIX
FRESH NEGLIGENCE

John and I sat in our car looking at the modest hospital. Since our meeting with the surgeon John had become totally silent. I think in his own heart he was strengthening his resolve for what lay ahead. We knew the odds were not in his favor, but like me, we prayed continuously for divine intervention.

As we walked toward the building, the sunny day and a light breeze combined to challenge our pessimism. For the second time in my life sitting with John in a hospital I had to put a smile on my face and hide my feelings of anguish.

When my mother was having a series of small strokes in her last year of life, she would call me sometimes in the middle of the night and implore me to come over to reassure her. At such times, I sat by her bed and smiled, telling her over and over she would be all right. Here again I was called upon to lie and suppress my fears in the face of an implacable enemy, death. She and I held hands and smiled at each other, but I knew she was dying. She didn't want to talk about it.

Now here again, I knew John was going to die—I knew it completely and honestly. I didn't know how it would happen, but the pit of ice in my stomach was growing telling me my anticipation was correct. Would he make it through the operation or die in the aftermath? Or would he make it through the operation, but die of complications? I certainly never anticipated what actually happened.

We pushed open the large glass doors and stepped inside the building. We went immediately to the admissions office where John sat quietly as I answered endless questions.

The surgeon prescribed for John a procedure called "bronchoscopy". It was the direct visual examination of the tracheobronchial tree by using a flexible tube containing light-transmitting glass fibers that return a magnified image. John had to be pre-medicated with atropine morphine. A small dose of anesthesia was sprayed into his mouth, throat and tongue and then through the nose. A nasal catheter was placed through the nostril down to the avula. A Lidocaine jelly was used as a lubricant to protect John's mucosa from the Fiberbronchoscope that could cause abrasion. Then the scope was introduced through the nose or mouth and pushed down to the epiglottis where more anesthesia of the glottis would be completed. So they blocked both his nose and his mouth. Imagine, the discomfort of trying to breathe. This test also carries with it the danger that the patient could go into cardiac arrest, hemorrhage, have lack of breath or experience spasms of the throat. This procedure also gives the patient mild bronchitis afterward. The patient's swallowing and cough reflexes are depressed for an hour or so.

The reason for this graphic description of a procedure is to show you what the government, the architects and the installers of asbestos at Biscayne Annex Post Office were putting John through by building a death trap and loading it with asbestos. It is also included to show people who are willing to accept a horrible test without knowing just what is done. In that way you will understand the pain and torture they put you through. But this test was just a preliminary test. Imagine how people suffer during these procedures! Most of the time you are unaware of the trauma because they come back to their rooms either asleep or smiling to make loved ones feel better.

When the surgeon described this procedure, he did not tell John what it entailed, just that "it provided a closer look at the lesion in the lung." Even the doctor who conducted the test did not tell John what to expect. They just told him it had to be done, and gave him no choice in the matter. They never told him his throat and nose would be invaded and eventually the bronchial tubes leading down to his lung. The fog of the infection that was obscuring the lesion had to be penetrated. The results would give the surgeon a clear picture of how the operation should proceed, if needed. He decided the pneumonia should be treated with inhalation therapy to cut down on the complications of surgery, if performed.

Pangs of sympathy for my darling's discomfort during that terrible test were the first hurdle to overcome. I was taking it one step at a time. Time seemed to slow down as each new hurdle arose.

A very important thing happened at this point. The admissions receptionist asked me if John had any allergies. I remember being quite emphatic to her. "Yes," I said, "he is terribly allergic to allergens including common soap. He cannot even shower with anything but a non-soap product." I told her he could have an allergic reaction to most anything. Didn't anyone ever look on John's chart to see this abnormality? I doubt whether this condition was even <u>noted</u> on his chart and on his wristband. It should have been for the staff and doctors. It was the first omission that actually caused John's death.

We were shown to a private room on the cancer floor. There was immediate activity around John as soon as he undressed and climbed into bed. The inhalation therapist came in and started John on his treatments. There was medication in the machine, which had a tube that fit into John's mouth. He was to inhale as much of the medication as he could before exhaling. The medication was to decrease the infection in his lungs and clear away the pneumonia.

Of course blood was drawn and specimens taken. John had to be thinking of that time long ago when they had fed acid through his veins to his brain. This time the outcome of the risky procedure was just as uncertain.

The resident doctor appeared, along with the doctor who would conduct the procedure the next day. John was not to eat or drink anything after midnight.

Now that actions were being taken, I relaxed somewhat. I felt everything was out of our hands and into the hands of the professionals.

I had my Masters degree in psychology by that time, and I thought it was my role to keep John's spirits up. It would only be natural for depression to settle in under the circumstances. I knew the mind could do great harm to the body if John began to slip into sadness or fear.

At this point, all the nurses and aides devoted themselves to making John comfortable. He seemed to be less distant and conversed and laughed more often.

Our friend, who was still alive but completely disabled by her illness, had become aware of her lung cancer on the morning she suddenly started coughing up blood. A lifelong cigarette smoker, she was amazed that she could be hiding lung cancer without feeling any changes in her body. Even when she saw this first serious sign of its existence she refused to believe it.

After the inhalation treatment, John started to spit up blood. His ashen face looked stricken. He was now no longer capable of hiding behind his denial when he saw the blood. I sat on the bed with him and talked myself blue in the face trying to convince him the blood was due to the pneumonia inhalation treatments. "It's proof of the congestion breaking up," I insisted. He finally seemed to accept that logic and fell asleep.

I was very pleased with the choice of John's surgeon. He was small but mighty—a dynamo. I knew how very smart he was after checking his education and credentials. His reassurance was probably the main reason John accepted his instructions so calmly.

While I was waiting for John to wake up, I experienced a wave of anxiety when I became aware of a stranger standing at the door to the room. The stranger was abrupt and exuded an air of casualness and breeziness, which I thought was out of place in a sick room. He took a chair and introduced himself as the surgeon's partner. He tried to minimize the bad news he had to tell us. He crossed his leg over his knee revealing wild, red patterned sox. I didn't like those inappropriate sox and I didn't like his manner.

John was awake now so the doctor addressed his remarks to John and ignored me. It seemed the first surgeon was on a convention and this doctor, his partner, was taking over John's case for the time being. No one had consulted with us about this change in personnel. My disappointment in the first surgeon's disappearance was palpable.

This new man related to John what he could expect from the scheduled test. His explanation was sketchy and vague. He said it would be short and without too much discomfort. I remember wondering if he had ever had the test himself. If not, how could he predict that it would be "short and without discomfort?" He neglected to mention the nitty-gritty procedure and whether it would be alarming for John psychologically or emotionally. He gave the impression of arrogance, impatience, and, (like many surgeons) a messianic attitude. Then he popped up abruptly and was gone even before we had a chance to react to all this information. I had a terrible premonition about this man, sharpened by my psychological education on reading people. I would have put up a fuss if he had told me the first surgeon was not going to do the operation, but he didn't tell us.

The next day John endured the test. He came back looking ashen and pale, but did not complain. The results came quickly— they would have to do another test. This one, I have to believe was a thoracoscopy. This time an incision was made at the base of John's throat where an instrument was introduced to "explore the lung." A biopsy may have been taken too. This means the lung has to be deflated and then inflated again. This test was much more serious and dangerous. After this test, John came back shaken with discomfort from the gash across his throat.

I knew this procedure indicated that the infection was worse than they thought and hard to see through. John got fidgety in the bed and looked like a trapped animal. We did not hear from either surgeon so I can only assume they were content to leave the bad news in the hands of the doctor who would be performing the test. I thought this cowardly, but said nothing to John.

In the morning they took him down the long corridors to the operating room. It was hours before they brought him back. He was alert but silent. He had a long slash across his throat, one that would normally have taken weeks to heal thoroughly. I finally got it out of him that the test was uncomfortable but he refused any painkillers. After the test, the partner to the surgeon appeared again.

The lesion was cancerous and had to come out! The first surgeon would not do the operation, the partner would. I protested long and loud. I wanted our first surgeon to do the operation, thank you very much. I said we would wait until he was available. The second surgeon seemed surprised and somewhat angry. He gave me a short version of his credentials and his years of dealing with such cancers. He said it was imperative and in the best interest of my husband that he be allowed to proceed. Time was of the essence and the first surgeon would not be available for some time. He was treating me like some airhead who didn't see the need for promptness.

I hated the first surgeon at this point for putting us into this position, and I didn't trust his arrogant partner. I thought he was knife-happy and cavalier lumping John with his thousands of cases. I had many bad feelings about this decision and I know now I was right. In the end we left the decision up to John. He wanted the ordeal over with and it was easy to understand why. Either he would have his life back, and be comparably normal, or he would not make it. It was in God's hands now and he agreed with the second surgeon that he wanted it done as soon as possible. Could I argue in the face of that plea? It was settled. That night I called for a priest. John and I both took communion. That night my husband was feeling better. His fever was down and his lungs were almost clear. He felt optimally well. We had a pleasant evening together.

In the morning, they took John down to surgery early. The poor man had been living on broth and crackers and Jell-o. Once again he could have nothing to eat or drink after midnight. John's sister, Theresa, had come down from Cleveland, and his brother, Tony was there. John Jr., Sam and I all paced the waiting room during the long hours we waited. The surgeon said the operation would take around four hours. Soon it was six hours and no John.

With every tick of the clock I felt my time with my husband drawing to a close. As I sat waiting for news I had already begun the grievance process—the fifth stage of separation and emptiness. I have never felt so completely helpless and alone before or since.

At long last, the surgeon was there in his green scrubs. The family closed around him while he described the operation. They had to take the lower half of John's right lung along with part of the sac that surrounded the heart, and some of his bronchial tube. The cancer was quite advanced, so it had been growing for a long time, and had started to move out of the lung and into the surrounding areas. The surgeon was optimistic that he had gotten it all. There was no sign of any cancer in his left lung. At this point I had the presence of mind to ask him to have the lung tissue tested for asbestos. The surgeon looked at me in surprise and disbelief. However, he said he would make the request. Our family members sighed collectively in happiness that the operation was over. Though they were disturbed at how advanced the cancer had been, it seemed that the enemy had been defeated. Our side had won.

We waited an hour to see John. They had him propped up in bed in a fresh gown. He looked sheepish, but happy. I ran to his bed and he allowed me to hug him gently. His hospital gown was opened in the back. When I saw the incision that ran the full length of his back and around part of his waist I cried out in my thoughts, <u>Dear God, what have they done to him?</u> There had to be at least fifty staples closing the wound. The pain he must have endured had to be deep and intense. Yet, John refused painkillers in front of the family. I found out later from the nurses that after we left, he did agree to take some medication for the pain. We stayed with him for half an hour. In that time he was exuberant, joking and relaxed. He was the old John, staples and all.

For the next two days the family visited every day. John was up walking around, shaving, using the bathroom on his own, and eating huge meals. He was happy again and looking forward to going back to work.

His cubicle was covered on every wall with cards and letters from friends and co-workers. Nurses told me what a wonderful patient he was. The surgeon told us he would be moving John back to a private room the next day. "He is making a miraculous recovery," he said. Life was good. The sun was out again. I even found that arrogant surgeon tolerable.

One moment of clouds occurred when John put his hand under my chin and looked me straight in the eyes. "What if it comes back, or it shows up in the other lung?" He asked. He wanted to judge for himself how strongly I believed in his recovery by watching my face.

I smiled and gave him a big kiss. "Don't be looking for trouble. The surgeon said he got it all, and I believe him. We'll just take one day at a time and leave it up to God." I hugged him tightly and felt him relax.

HE WAS WELL, HAPPY AND MAKING A SPEEDY RECOVERY. ALL HIS VITAL SIGNS WERE NORMAL. THE DOCTORS ALL PRONOUNCED HIM OUT OF DANGER AND URGED US TO GET ON WITH OUR LIVES. THE DOCTOR'S OATH SAYS DO NO HARM.

I'll never forget one nurse. On that second day of John's recuperation from surgery she stopped me on my way out.

"He's a wonderful man," she said. "It's a joy to be around him and look at all those cards and letters. You're lucky to have him."

She patted me on the shoulder as I thanked her and walked away wondering why the ice in my stomach would not go away.

CHAPTER SEVEN
COMBINED NEGLIGENCE

On the third day out of surgery, John was well on the road to recovery. He was walking around, laughing, eating well, sitting up most of the day in a chair, and refusing pain medication. After my morning visit, he seemed restless to go back to his private room. He talked about how they needed him back at work. I could always tell, when John became eager to get back to work, he was also ready to get back into life.

When I returned for my evening visit, my sister-in-law, Theresa, was already there. She had spent the day with John and had gone down to the cafeteria for a quick snack. I walked into intensive care and found John seated in a chair beside an IV stand. The first thing I became aware of as I walked from the cool hall into the large, intensive care room was the overpowering heat that hit me in the face as I entered. The temperature was sweltering. I sat down across from John and asked him what was going on?

"The air conditioning is broken," he explained. I could see his face was flushed a bright red. I got up and walked to the nurses' station. She was fanning herself with a chart for a little relief.

"What the heck is happening? This is terrible." I commented.

She put down the chart.

"It's been like this all day. They're working on it."

"It must be above a hundred degrees in here," I persisted. "This can't be very comfortable for the patients just after surgery. This is a disgrace. Has the surgeon been in to see John?"

She looked in John's chart and said the surgeon had been in and had written orders.

"Well, I hope they get this fixed soon, John's looking uncomfortable."

I walked away and sat down across from John again. Then I noticed something I hadn't seen the first time. My husband's IV bottle held blood! I watched as the blood flowed into John's veins. He was getting a transfusion. I was immediately shocked and distressed.

"Why are they giving you blood?" I said in a calm voice but inside I was angry.

"The surgeon ordered two pints. He said he wanted to build up my cell count."

TWO PINTS! I could tell he wasn't happy, but was still accepting all that was done to him without question.

I couldn't control my disbelief. "You were just operated on for lung cancer. Blood transfusions are dangerous." I was thinking about the scare of late over the blood supply with the advent of AIDS. The blood supply had been tainted—it was in the news. "Why didn't he ask a member of our family to give you fresh blood?"

John shrugged, "I don't know. God, it's hot in here. It's been like this all day."

I could see he was sweating. I brought him some tissues and, for the first time, I vented my stored up anger.

"They shouldn't be giving you blood," I exclaimed. "They should have asked our family if they wanted to give you blood. Besides, this heat could taint that blood. I told them you were allergic to everything. I can't believe the surgeon would take a chance giving you blood when you have just lost half a lung. Even if there is only one chance in a trillion that something could happen, he's supposed to know blood transfusions are dangerous."

John shrugged again. "He just said he wanted to build up my cell count."

"I know—but there's nothing <u>wrong</u> with your cell count. He shouldn't take such chances. You're doing great. And he ordered two pints? That's <u>crazy</u>. He should have started with a test amount because of your allergies."

When I saw John frown I stopped. He was at the end of his second pint of blood. I sat there and watched the last pint go into my husband in a stifling room, blood he didn't need. If I had been there when the surgeon had come in I could have saved John's life by refusing the blood. But, I had to just sit there and watch my husband being killed.

When Theresa came back at the end of visiting hours she and I left together. She was staying at our house and all the way home in the car she complained about the hot room and the blood. She echoed my fears. We two women were not doctors but we knew, through common sense, that John should never have been given the blood from the hospital blood bank when they had fresh donors available in our family. And they never should have given it in such a hot room because heat can taint blood. Finally, they should never have given it to a patient whose cell count was good, and who had allergies to everything.

That night at about 10:00 p.m., John called me. I was relieved to hear him sound so normal. It was the first time he had called me from intensive care. He said he wanted me to bring a few things the next day. He said he was feeling good. The last thing he said to me was, "I'll see you in the morning." I had answered, "Yes, I'll see you in the morning, love."

I now know I was repeating the 30th Psalm, 5th verse. I was saying it to John because I would never again talk to him clearly on this Earth: "Crying may last for a night, but joy comes in the morning." It was our promise to each other that we would see each other again in heaven. It meant that I would cry for him in the darkness of my long night of grief, but I would have joy in the morning of our reunion, promised by God through his word. I have always clung to that promise. The closer I get to my own death, the larger it looms before me, and the more keenly I understand that it is true. I said I would see John in the morning, and I will. However, it wasn't the <u>next</u> morning.

Next morning when I arrived home from work the hospital called. I was to come immediately! The operator wouldn't tell me over the phone what had happened, only that I must come <u>"right now</u>." My icy stomach became a glacier of fear. I yelled to Theresa and my daughter-in-law to follow me in their car. I couldn't wait for anyone. I flew through traffic, parked at the main entrance to the hospital and ran through the long corridors, whispering under my breath all the time, "Please God, please God, <u>no</u>."

I found John in intensive care on a respirator. They had sedated him heavily. He was looking around desperately through drug-dazed eyes. I watched the machine yanking his chest up and down and thought of the fifty stitches he had down his body. How that must have pained him. The machine made an obscene noise. I wanted to put my hands over my ears to shut it out. I soon found my whole family by the bed asking questions I couldn't answer. Neither of John's two surgeons were anywhere to be seen.

I could tell all by myself, from my medical studies to get my Masters degree in psychology, that John had gone into Anaphylactic shock from the blood he was given. It was either not his type, or had been tainted by the overpowering heat in the room the day before. It was exactly what I had feared would happen.

The nurse told me John had started to have a hard time breathing about a half-hour after he hung up from our call. Neither the hospital nor the doctors had called me to come in when it happened. He had been suffering for nine long hours before they called and robbed me of precious time with my husband.

They had not been able to find the two surgeons to ask them what should be done. The resident doctor tried to explain. Nothing made sense. They had robbed me of precious time with my lover and made us sit in the waiting room. I could see John for only five minutes every hour.

They have never told us what happened. The resident doctor talked in riddles to cover their actions, never mentioning the blood. I told that resident over and over it was the blood and the heat that sent him into shock because he was allergic. He would nod but never talk to me about it. <u>It was maddening</u>! He kept ordering us not to go home. "These things happen," he said, "to someone just out of surgery. It looks bad." I asked to be allowed to sit with him but the doctor refused. They kept us out of the unit all day and all night.

Anaphylactic shock is "an acute, explosive systemic reaction characterized by respiratory distress, and vascular collapse." It occurs in sensitized people, like John, who has allergies, when given an antigen they are allergic to. In other words, John had an allergic shock to the blood. The vast amount of blood he was given insured his death. I have always felt that blood was either not of his blood group or it was tainted by the heat.

Negligence on the part of the blood department who matched the blood, or the hospital for allowing blood to be given when the air conditioning was out, stood out in bold relief. It had taken more than two hours for that blood to drain into John—time enough for it to become tainted by the heat.

In my estimation it was also negligence on the part of the surgeons. They ordered two pints of blood, when John was just out of surgery, without testing to see if he was allergic to it.

The hospital was negligent for not asking the family's permission to give John blood, and negligent for not getting fresh blood from the family members who were available at all times.

John's allergies should have been noted on his identification wristband, upon his admission. If it was not there, it was pure negligence on the part of the admitting clerk.

The hospital, its staff and specifically the surgeons killed John by their negligence. The hospital was culpable for the above reasons. The doctors were at fault for ordering the fatal blood transfusion after he was still weak from a major operation. They were guilty of not reading his admission information to find out if he were allergic. Allowing him to be transfused when the air conditioning was out and not asking for fresh blood from the family was negligence of the worst kind.

Sure, they tried to blame it on the operation. But the fact that John had the reaction six hours after receiving the blood pinpoints the cause. As soon as the tainted blood began circulating into his system his vascular system and respiratory system started to shut down.

The doctors told us to stay and not leave because they knew exactly how long it would take John to die. If that is not proof of negligence I don't know what is. They knew the blood was the cause his death was going to be the affect.

Type I shock occurred when the blood reached John's circulatory system. So say all the medical books. The most common cause is "foreign serum." Someone in the blood lab gave John blood foreign to his own; or the blood was curdled in the heat of the room. At the very least, a full-blown investigation should have been instituted to find out the cause for the shock. There was no question about that. He was obviously in shock.

Here's what happened to my lover: the smooth muscles contracted, veins dilated and the blood seeped into tissues and caused a decrease in blood volume. This caused the shock. Fluid escaped into John's lungs and caused pulmonary edema, the filling up of the lungs with fluid. John drowned in his own fluids. His heart went into cardiac arrest.

In typical cases, the patient complains of uneasiness and becomes agitated and flushed within 15 minutes. The nurses' notes in Johns record indicate he did just that. He complained of uneasiness, he became agitated and then flushed. John had been already flushed as he was receiving the blood. A small part of the reaction could have started at that time. It took six hours for the "remedy" to turn into full-blown shock but once it started, he was doomed. He must have been slightly agitated when he called me, but did not mention it. I think he called me because he was feeling uneasy and just wanted to hear my voice.

He soon suffered heart palpitations, numbness, throbbing in the ears, coughing, sneezing and difficulty breathing. He had all those symptoms. Cardiovascular collapse took over. All the veins and arteries to his heart shut down. He could have become convulsive. He did become unresponsive and then he died. It's all in his medical chart. It was not a pretty way to die.

Why didn't the medical professionals first test him with a small amount? Then if he had gone into shock, it would not have been so severe. Immediate treatment with epinephrine would have rescued him.

The use of epinephrine tells me the staff was fully aware he was in Anaphylactic shock. They are responsible. Nothing else could have caused this reaction. John was not taking any drugs for pain. A poisonous insect had not bitten him. No, they killed him with the blood. Their negligence is obvious. I will know that for the rest of my life.

On the evening of John's death they tried to tell us that it was from the operation, but that couldn't be true. Even the arrogant surgeon said it was "probably from the blood." John was having no complications from the surgery that would have sent him into Anaphylactic shock. Only an allergic substance could do it. He had only the blood. An allergic reaction requires an antigen, something you're allergic to. He was not allergic to the operation or anything they did during the operation. This diagnosis was their way of trying to erase their liability. John died of collapsed blood pressure and vascular collapse, the very malady his doctors had inserted wires into his chest to monitor.

JOHN'S DOCTORS LIED WHEN THEY PUT CAUSE OF DEATH ON HIS DEATH CERTIFICATE. They wrote "lesion of the right lung," blaming it on his cancer.

That certainly couldn't have been the cause of death. The lesion theory is nonsense. John was in the midst of a wonderfully fast recovery from the surgery. His doctors were scared to death of a lawsuit for negligence so they simply lied. The death certificate should have read, "Anaphylactic shock caused by foreign serum, blood."

It took John exactly twenty-four hours to die. Twenty-four hours of violent headaches, heart arrhythmia, loss of fluids, drowning in fluids in his lungs that stopped him from breathing, and his lungs and heart giving out. He was right on time; it usually takes twenty-four hours in serious reactions for the patient to die. It took John exactly that amount of time.

Much can be done to save a person suffering severe shock, but no doctor has ever gone over John's records to determine if everything possible was done. Once shock had started in my husband's body his doctors went into their own shock.

I had one talk with the resident. He did not tell me what they were doing. That was in the morning, and would you believe it—we did not see the surgeon until that evening, a full ten hours after John went into shock. We were treated like lepers, hidden away in the waiting room where no other person was allowed in. We were not allowed to go into the intensive care unit except for the prescribed five minutes each hour when all the staff disappeared so we couldn't ask questions of them. The only thing the surgeon told us, was, "Don't go home because John is going to die." He knew exactly how long it would take him to die because he knew John was having an allergic reaction and was in Anaphylactic shock.

In one of my five-minute visits, I reached over the bars of the bed and took John's hand. I leaned down and over the noise of the ventilator I said, "John, I love you so much." To my surprise, he squeezed my hand, and with great effort he told me clearly and plainly, even with the respirator tube down his throat, "I love you, too." These were his last words.

Somehow our family got through those twenty-four hours. Each of us took turns seeing John for those precious five minutes. At 11:00 p.m. that night, Theresa and I sat alone, dealing with our own shock. I suddenly heard "Code Blue." Someone was dead. They were trying to resuscitate whoever it was. Theresa got up, walked down to the door and looked into Intensive Care. She came back and said, in her denial, "It wasn't John." I relaxed. But, later I found that it <u>was</u> John! A nurse came to us ten minutes later and told us John was dead. Not the two surgeons, just a nurse. At no time did those two surgeons ever appear to tell us how sorry they were. From that moment on they were nowhere to be found.

We sat numb. I sank, despairing, into myself. I didn't talk, I couldn't think. I had no tears. I only felt numbness. I felt a cold wind blow across my heart. Real pain seized all my muscles. I calmly got up and went to the nurse who was in the hall. "I want to see John," I said.

She looked into my eyes and must have realized that he was ours now. Their five-minute ban was ended. I waited. They brought me into his cubicle. They had taken all the machines away. They had him raised slightly in the bed. My husband's face was peaceful. He appeared to be asleep. I bent over and kissed his mouth then laid my head on his shoulder. Theresa came in and kissed him.

The rest of the family arrived to say their good-byes. And then we had to let him go. Our temporal separation had begun.

What started with the government, the architect, the state and federal inspectors, and the installers, continued with the hospital staff, technicians, along with those two incompetent surgeons, their combined negligence had murdered my husband, John.

CHAPTER EIGHT
COVER-UPS

My husband's funeral was a blur. I wandered around in shock wearing John's bedroom slippers, which were miles too big for me. I refused to take them off, so I wore them everywhere, day and night. It was a sign of my non-acceptance that John was dead.

Sam had arranged for his friend, a psychiatrist, to come over and evaluate me. To my surprise the doctor offered me a job in his office. He assured me I was doing quite well. Secretly, he told Sam that a job in his office would allow him to monitor me for depression. He could then squeeze in therapy sessions as needed, without raising my suspicions. For some reason, I readily agreed to work for him.

When the funeral was over and relatives had gone back to Cleveland, Sam and his new wife, Kim, came to stay with me. They stayed a whole year until they were sure I was functioning well, and ready to get on with my life.

As time passed, my grief subsided but not my anger. I knew the hospital had been negligent, along with the doctors. I wanted to find out what John's legal rights were in a lawsuit. My attorney had drawn up John's will, but did not do wrongful death cases. At the time, I was completely ignorant about the law and how to deal with lawyers.

The first lawyer I went to was tied to officials at the office where I had worked. I made an appointment with this firm and took John's will along with me for them to look at.

The offices were paneled in dark wood and appeared gloomy. Still, there was a great deal of activity going on there. I felt they must have a booming business. The firm specialized in compensation cases for accidents and offered contingency arrangements. "Contingency" means they would take the case if they thought they could make money with it. If I did get any settlement monies, they would take 40% of the settlement. If they had to go to trial they would get 50% and I would get 50%. I thought that was pretty straightforward. I know now that was a standardized agreement for such a case.

The first lawyer, whose name escapes me, took me into his office and invited me to sit down across from his desk. "Now, Mrs. Zocco, what can I do for you?" He asked it kindly.

He was a large man with a beard, and he was poised over a legal yellow pad, ready to write down my every word.

I proceeded to tell him the story of the hospital, the blood and the doctors. I presented him with John's will, and the death certificate. He had been busy as a bee writing the details, but suddenly he had stopped writing.

"Look, LaVerne," he advised, "I can't do anything until I have a look at John's hospital records. You have to provide those to me. Just go down to the hospital record department and get copies. Bring me the copies and I'll look them over. No reason to go into any agreements now. I'll also have a look at John's will and see what we have to do there."

I was disappointed that he wouldn't tell me about what constituted a case of wrongful death against the hospital and the doctors. Had I known then what I know now, I would have insisted on a much more in-depth discussion. I think I would now be able to spot an experienced and enthusiastic advocate for my side. It made sense that they would want to see the records, but he was making me do all the work. A lawyer should be able to judge by what you tell him if you have a good case or not, and he should believe what you tell him. I'm sure this lawyer sized me up as being "a poor widow who was in the throes of grief" and was surely exaggerating.

"When you have the records, come on back and I'll see you immediately," he assured me. He shook my hand and left the room. Somehow, I felt more alone than ever. He hadn't told me I had a good case. He hadn't commiserated with me about the death of my husband. He hadn't expressed his concern over what had been done to John. He hadn't consoled me in any way. He had thrown everything back into my lap to proceed alone.

I was disappointed but not discouraged. When I got home I called the hospital and talked to a clerk in the records department. He was very cooperative. For ninety-eight dollars they would copy the records and send them to me.

It took about three weeks to get them but they finally came. I noticed that it was not John's complete record. All his admission paperwork and all notes made before the operation had been culled. They included only the records of the surgery and the records of his death. There was no mention of his being given blood, or the possibility of tainted blood, or the heat of the Intensive Care Unit. What it did contain was an hour-by-hour report of his going into shock, but no mention of Anaphylactic shock. Everything that had been done was noted in medical terms. At the end, the conclusion was documented that he had died from a lesion to his right lung and that was what was certified on his death certificate. Adding insult to injury, the lab report from the pathologist stated there were no asbestos fibers in his lungs.

With the records in hand I made another appointment to see the lawyer.

Several times a week I worked for the psychiatrist. I helped him fill out insurance forms and write letters to judges and lawyers about legal testimony. I acted as an intern and consultant to him. He would fill me in on certain circumstances of particular cases, without telling me the client's name, and I would tell him my initial impressions of the client's mental processes. If he were unsatisfied with my answer, he would make me get a book on the subject from his library and read up on the topic. Far from being annoyed, I was thrilled by his mentoring. He taught me a vast amount of knowledge I had never come across in school, even for my Master degree.

The psychiatrist also worked as a consulting psychiatrist to an established drug and alcohol clinic. Once a week he saw their new clients and drew up profiles for each one, detailing their mental aspects. I was very interested in this branch of the field. He allowed me to study the paperwork the clients filled out so we could discuss how he drew his assumptions based on accepted developmental doctrine.

About every second visit he would sit me down for a mini-session. He had prescribed for me an excellent anti-depressant medication to bring me up out of my depressed mood. In a few months we did away with them altogether.

"How are you feeling today?" He would always ask at the opening of each session. One day I told him the following scenario:

"I had a dream the other night about John. We were on a cruise ship and I had left the ship to investigate the island where the ship was moored. I had left John sleeping in the stateroom. I remember getting panicky and calling John from a phone booth on the dock. He told me he couldn't be with me right now, and that I would have to get used to exploring without him. As I watched in terror, the ship pulled away from the dock and sailed away until it was out of sight. The phone went dead and I just watched and cried."

I destroyed several tissues from the box on the table and wiped my flowing tears as I smiled at the doctor.

"You don't have to interpret the dream for me," I continued. "John sleeping on the ship and me on the shore means parted by his death. He was telling me I had to get on with my life without him. The ship sailing away means he's gone forever and I won't see him anymore. Now I have to explore life alone."

The psychiatrist seemed to be impressed.

"Sam told me something that made me face up to reality and accept it," I continued. "He said, 'he isn't coming back, mom.' I know he's right but it's still very hard to deal with. My head says it's what I have to do, but my heart says <u>not so fast</u>."

The doctor leaned forward with an understanding look on his face. "How did you make out with his annuity from the Post Office?" He asked.

Waves of anger swept over me. "John thought I would get half of his retirement pay if anything happened to him. If he had still been under Social Security I would have. I would have gotten around eight hundred dollars a month. But, because he died prior to being eligible to retire, they penalized me. I get only half of a half, four hundred dollars. It's not much after having his whole check to live on. There is no arguing with them. After all the monies he put in for twenty-four long years. What a rip off."

The doctor shook his head in sympathy.

"Are you going to be able to make it?"

"You're the first one to ask me that question," I replied. "I'll make it but not with any help from the Post Office. I do get a widow's pension under Social Security that makes up some of the difference, but not all. He left me minimum life insurance, but we had savings bonds, and the house is paid for. I think I'll be okay. It's not for the money I'm trying to get a lawyer to do something. It's the injustice of it all."

"What about your case against the hospital and doctors? What's new there?"

I shook my head. "I received his hospital records to bring to the lawyer this afternoon, and they're only a partial record. I gave him John's will the last time I saw him. I guess it will take another couple of days while they study the records."

"What else is going on?"

"I called the Post Office insurance department and found out I can file a wrongful death compensation claim for federal benefits with the Workmen's Compensation office in Jacksonville. I have to find out about this asbestos thing from someone. I'm in the dark where to start. I guess it will have to be one or the other. Either the hospital killed him with their negligence, or the government killed him with their negligence. I don't know if I can sue both. Actually, they were both at fault. The asbestos caused the lung cancer, but the blood sent him into the shock that killed him. First I have to give the lawyers these records. Then we'll go from there. Whatever happens, I have only two years to file a suit, the lawyers tell me. The law imposes a Statute of Limitations. You wouldn't think there would be limitations on murder."

My friend sighed. "Maybe you shouldn't get your hopes up too high," he replied. "You have a good view of people's honesty but don't forget, you're talking money now. People change when money is involved, especially lawyers."

"You don't think they can deny they killed John?" I demanded. "The hospital's records show it was shock."

"I'm just saying don't get too hopeful. And be careful of lawyers and what you sign."

That afternoon I took the records to the lawyer. He was very busy and asked me to leave them. He would get back to me in a few days. In about two weeks I was called into his office. He got right to the point.

"I've gone over the records," he began. "To sue a hospital or doctor, you have to prove not just that they were negligent, but that they were negligent with a malicious intent. It seems you may be right about the blood sending John into shock, but you would have to prove they did it intentionally, and that would be impossible to do.

"It was most likely an accident or an unintended mistake. The doctor was doing his job with good intentions. He ordered the blood because he was trying to be on the safe side. The air conditioning breaking down was no one's fault and they fixed it as soon as possible. The blood could have been mismatched through an error or the heat could have turned it bad, but it was not done maliciously. No, there is nothing here we can hang our hats on. As for the asbestos, the hospital's report shows that there were no fibers in John's lungs. The surgeon saying John had clubbed fingers without collaborating evidence of lung fibers seems to exclude asbestosis. Besides, that is a specialized illness and we don't handle that kind of case. I'm sorry but we will not take this case."

With that he handed me back the records. As I rose to go, I asked about John's will. He hurried out of the office to get it. When he came back he looked distressed. "I'm sorry," he apologized, "we seem to have lost John's will. If it turns up we'll mail it to you." With that he ushered me out of the office.

I walked around in a daze in the parking lot trying to find my car. I could hardly believe what he had told me. The hospital and doctors were going to get away with murder. I could sense that no law firm would take the case. Besides, it would cost too much money to prepare if they were not going to receive a lot of money in return.

At that moment, sitting in the car crying, with the warm Florida sun's rays glinting through the windshield, I realized the first truism about the law. The rightness of my claim that John had died of neglect and that someone in that hospital, along with the doctors, had caused that neglect did not guarantee that justice would be served. The lawyers were interested only in money. How much would this case bring in, compared to how much they would have to pay out, that was the bottom line. They may agree that what happened to John was horrible and unfair. They may agree he should have his day in court, to hear his murderers confess their great sins. But if that justice did not bring with it big bucks, forget it. They were not interested in pursuing the <u>right</u> thing, only the <u>lucrative</u> thing. It may make me feel better to have closure on the murder so that I could get on with my life, but that was not what the courts were for. The courts make lawyers money by threat of revealing culpability. Money is more important than pinpointing truth. The truth did not make money.

I know now they should have filed this case and argued with the hospital's insurance company. Because there were many truths on our side, supported by the record, there was enough ammunition for a good case with or without proving malice in their negligence. This lawyer was wrong. He had cost John his day in court by telling me I had no case. Unfortunately, I believed him.

I never again pursued the avenue of appeal against the hospital or doctors, thinking I had no chance of prevailing. Down the line many lawyers would ask me why I did not pursue this part of the case. My answer always was, "I believed the lawyer." They would all shake their heads at me and wonder at my gullibility.

That afternoon I called the arrogant surgeon. I told him he and the hospital had not done the right things for John. I told him he should have read John's admission information and he would have found out he was allergic to everything. I said he should not have ordered two pints of blood, that it was way too much without testing it first. I accused him of knowing that the air conditioning was broken and the blood was tainted, and that John died of Anaphylactic shock in addition to the lesion on his right lung. I said surgeons buried their mistakes and charged that he had no right to have given John the blood if there was the tiniest chance it could cause a reaction. I said blood transfusions were dangerous under the best of circumstances.

He listened patiently, told me I was overwrought, a phrase I would hear many times in the next ten years. He said that even if I was right, nothing could be done now. He said he had been expecting my call and wondered why it had taken me so long. He said hindsight was always better than foresight and perhaps he should not have ordered the blood, but it was a "judgment call." He said he knew nothing of John's allergies, nothing about the room being hot or the tainting of the blood. Oh, he was smooth and plausible. He was going to retire and he wished me well.

He never once apologized for what had happened to John or talked of the pain John had gone through. He dismissed me as a gadfly, knowing full well there was no chance an investigation would be instituted.

The hospital was forced to go out of business and start as another entity after a series of bad publicity stories featured their neglect, in another case, for not providing safety measures. One of its doctors was shot to death by a disgruntled patient in the psychiatric ward. The hospital still exists but as a second-rate neighborhood hospital.

As for John's will, the lawyers never found it! I had to ask the lawyer who drew it up to give me the original. They refused and would only give me a copy. Luckily, it did not have to go through probate since everything was in both John's and my name. But, down the line I had to have a lawyer draw up papers appointing me John's legal representative so I could sign legal papers and checks from the post office for his sick time and vacation time. It caused me great inconvenience and more money to make up for that first lawyer's carelessness.

Whenever I think of that first lawyer, I don't think of the money he cost me. I only think about his false advice. I think of the information he suppressed—information that might have led to justice and closure. Without that, I was destined to seek them in other quarters.

CHAPTER NINE
THE MISSING COMPENSATION

The Federal Workmen's Compensation Act is a fraud. It is a program administered <u>against</u> the injured or dead employee. It is a program set up by Congress for the express purpose of keeping federal employees, injured or killed on the job by government stupidity, from suing the government. It is a bogus system that makes its own rules as it goes along. Oh, they have rules, all right, but they don't follow them. There isn't a lawyer in Florida who will take a case involving the WCO (Workmen's Compensation Office) located in Jacksonville, Florida because they know the office is set up to deny claims and if they lose cases they will not pay attorneys' fees.

A bulletin created by the Department of Labor who is responsible for carrying out the mandates of the FWCA (Federal Workers' Compensation Act), hangs in every government facility. It gives instructions about how an employee can claim benefits and the proper way to do so. However, it does not address what happens when the injury is lung cancer brought on by exposure to asbestos in a governmental workplace condemned as inundated with lethal type asbestos fibers that can cause lung cancer or asbestosis. It does not offer compensation when it takes twenty-three years for the cancer to show itself, which the medical field agrees is the length of time it takes such a cancer to grow after exposure. It does not give widows instructions about how to file claims, or even where to get the forms. The word "death" is mentioned one time in small print at the bottom of the page. So obviously they are supposed to give death benefits. The only thing they don't say is that they will not do so.

The day government officials shut down the Biscayne Annex they confessed that the asbestos contained therein could cause asbestosis and/or lung cancer but they never notified the public or the postal employees that they might develop these illnesses, even die from them. And they never said what employees should do or what the public should do if they developed these symptoms, even if it took twenty to forty years for them to appear.

John never had a chance to tell a supervisor he had lung cancer. By the time we knew he had lung cancer, he was in the hospital, operated on, then dead. We had no time to file a claim while he was alive, or see a government doctor in a government hospital to document his case. Moving from discovery, to operation, to death, took one week.

The very fact that the government shut down the Biscayne Annex is proof that the government was liable for negligence that resulted in asbestosis or lung cancer that developed in the employees or in the public. The very fact that John's co-worker had a lung removed while working there, (as did John), shows they worked in the most dangerous part of the building and it was no coincidence. The WCO turned his friend down for benefits "because she smoked cigarettes" denying any responsibility. That should have told us what monsters we would be dealing with. I was entitled to half of John's pay until the day I died. I was entitled to burial fees, medical bills, and a $10,000 grant. In all, over this fourteen-year period since John's death, it amounts to at least a million dollars and goes up each year I stay alive.

The WCO, (Workmen's Compensation Office) in Jacksonville, never contacted me to let me know I was entitled to file a claim as a widow of a civilian federal employee who had been killed by exposure to asbestos in a government building. Only through a lovely woman in the Post Office Personnel Office did I learn that I was entitled to the application. I was also entitled to have

John's union attorney handle the case, but I didn't know that at the time.

I also did not remember at the time that when the government condemned the building and moved all employees to the new airport facility they x-rayed every employee <u>except</u> John. Just imagine their negligence in x-raying all John's co-workers who worked in the same department as he did, in the same part of the building, and not x-ray John. That forbidden x-ray might have shown an early growth, and such early detection might have saved John's life.

I received the claim form, filled it out to the best of my knowledge and sent along John's medical records from the hospital but nothing from the two surgeons. In my reading of the Federal Workmen's Compensation Act, it was up to the WCO to get the statements from John's doctors, if they needed the data.

At this time I had already contacted a lawyer who was supposed to be an expert in asbestos cases. He had obtained samples of John's lung tissue and had sent them to Mt. Sinai Hospital in New York, where two of the most renowned asbestos doctors worked. It had to be sent to Mt. Sinai since they were the only hospital in the region that had an electronic microscope.

They both examined the tissue and under oath, and in front of a recording stenographer, signed depositions that John's lungs were full of asbestos fibers of combined lethal varieties: chrysotile, amonibole, and tremolite. That this lethal combination was found in the asbestos shipped in from Canada, and if this were true of the asbestos that was sprayed onto the walls and interior of the Biscayne Annex, it would be a perfect match to the fibers found in John's lungs. And since John was never exposed to asbestos anywhere else, and he was not a cigarette smoker, it would be irrefutable evidence that the lung cancer he developed was caused by his exposure in the workplace and that his death was wrongful.

What I sent to the WCO over time was the fact the Biscayne Annex had been shut down due to asbestos poisoning of the environment, and that John had been exposed to the asbestos for twelve and one-half years, but that it had taken twenty-three years for the cancer to show up. I also included that he had been diagnosed by the two surgeons, prior to going to the hospital, who had found the clubbed fingers of asbestosis, and a lesion on his right lung, and that John had died from the lesion on the right lung. I sent the death certificate and his medical records to the WCO office, but I did not send the records from the surgeon's examination thinking the WCO would do so to verify my statement.

I also sent to the WCO the two depositions from the Drs. At Mt. Sinai in New York, their sworn depositions. They both certified that it had been John's exposure to asbestos at the Biscayne Annex that had killed him. I sent my claim along with all this information in 1989-90 after my experience with John's union, which comes in the next chapter.

I thought the WCO would investigate the Biscayne Annex situation, and contact the surgeons and the two deposed doctors from Mt. Sinai. I thought this would take months and months. In the meantime I was in the midst of supplying information to our asbestos attorney for trial. I had no doubt that the WCO would find the government liable and approve my claim.

I sat back thinking the investigation would take a long time and I felt relieved to finally have John's death coming to closure by the acceptance of the federal government of its legitimate liability.

According to the Act of Congress setting up the FECA, it was intended to be remedial, and to proceed under a non-adversarial process. In other words, they were to be as helpful as possible, make the processing of claims as easy as possible, and pay the claims without contentious arguments. In reality, they do just the opposite. They do not help the claimant one bit. They do not make the claims process easy with individual attention. All transactions are done by mail without ever talking to the claimant in person. They hire their own experts to shoot down your case with biased testimony paid for by the government. This program is supposed to be for the employee and their survivors. It's supposed to be kind, benevolent and helpful. The money, for legitimate claims, is meant to replace the monies the victim might have earned had he/she not been exposed to the asbestos and died from lung cancer directly attributable to the government and the work environment it provided.

Non-adversarial means no lawyers or court proceedings. It is not to be like a court proceeding where a lawyer for the claimant is on one side with an opinion in favor of the claimant, and a lawyer is on the other side representing the government. Non-adversarial means the WCO was to investigate the claim, pay attention to medical records and testimony and depositions, pay attention to the fact the government had already conceded negligence by not x-raying John and by condemning his workplace as lethal. Based on the facts found in their investigations, they are to approve or disapprove the claim. This was not done.

A few weeks after filing, I was amazed to get a notice denying my claim on a form letter!

No investigation report was enclosed. There was no well-reasoned, well-thought-out consideration of the facts. No mention of the Biscayne Annex debacle was expressed, no mention of the asbestos, no mention of the findings of John's physicians or the two doctors from New York. Instead they gave a terse statement that <u>their</u> doctor (who the hell is he if this is non-adversarial?) had opined that John's lung cancer was not due to the asbestos, but due to cigarette smoking. This must be a standard song they sing to all cancer claimants to account for their lung cancer. This was the same reason they had given for turning down John's co-worker's claim. Only this time they were wrong.

Nowhere did they list their doctor's credentials as an expert in the asbestos field, because he had none. Nowhere did they give supportable evidence on how he came to his conclusion when no- where in the record did it say John was a cigarette smoker. Nowhere did they say how their doctor's opinion could possibly outweigh the testimony of the two experts from Mt. Sinai. The fact is he was a hired gun, hired by the government, to give fallacious and unsupported opinions to bar paying out claims.

I was stunned, to say the least. They gave me an attached form giving me information for asking for a hearing or review if I had new evidence. New Evidence? What happened to the evidence I had already submitted?

The office gave no reason for not crediting the doctors and reports and depositions. We were three to one against their doctor. The preponderance of evidence was on our side, yet they denied benefits based upon their doctor's opinion. Okay, so I thought they are just trying to make this harder. Their doctor could only have this one opinion as allowed in a court of law since they had instituted this illegal adversarial proceeding and he would have to stand by that one opinion. I was ready to go the extra mile and disprove his opinion. I might add, even my asbestos lawyer would not handle this case.

In my pea-brain, I thought if I could show their doctor's opinion was hot air then I would be awarded the benefits.

So, hateful as it was to me, I called the arrogant surgeon and asked him for a letter stating John was not a cigarette smoker, which John had verified to him. Though he smoked a pipe sporadically, that was attested to by his co-workers in depositions, he was at no time a cigarette smoker, and according to the New York doctor's supporting testimony, pipe smoking was irrelevant to the type cancer he had developed. To my everlasting relief the arrogant surgeon gave me such a letter. I sent the letter to the WCO as my new evidence fully confident I had removed the obstacle with which they had scotched me. I fully expected they would now get in contact with the surgeon and verify his opinion.

I also noticed that every time I was contacted now it was by a different person in the office, with a different title and position. You couldn't keep them straight.

This time they sent back another denial of the claim!

Remember, this is supposed to be a non-adversarial procedure. At no time did they tell me I would need a lawyer. They are supposed to investigate claims, not pick apart your claim, hoping to find some reason to turn you down.

Now, their doctor, with no credentials at all in the asbestos field, had the nerve to come forth with a second opinion, which he was not entitled to give. He is bound by law in a due process situation to stand by his first opinion for denying the claim. Instead, he changed his opinion now, and said that the asbestos that John had in his lungs was not the lethal kind. But this doctor had no electronic microscope. He had no Energy Dispersion Spectocopy. He was not an expert in asbestos with any degrees or credentials. He was nothing but a paid hired-gun quick to deny claims. It was an adversarial opinion designed to contradict John's surgeon, and the two doctors in New York. Usually a preponderance of evidence wins the day, but not with the WCO.

Their doctor had decided, that since the surgeon's opinion was that (and who should know better) John's pipe smoking could not cause the type of cancer he had his first opinion would not stand.

And so he gave himself another shot at it. Illegally.

Now, he said the asbestos reported was <u>not</u> lethal. He said nothing about our doctors' opinions, two experts in the field. He just gave his fallacious opinion in his ignorance and the WCO readily accepted it. He was not an asbestos expert. He had never seen the lung tissue. He did not mention the Biscayne Annex. He ignored his first opinion that was absolutely wrong. He was an adversary in a non-adversarial procedure, and he gave this opinion to stop me from receiving benefits. He took the view that chrysotile asbestos fiber was not considered lethal, but ignored the fact that the combination of chrysotile, amonibole and tremolite fibers were considered by the field to be very lethal. The Mt. Sinai doctor's article, supported by thirty-one other experts in the field, and part of his sworn deposition, laid out the current thinking of the field that indeed chrysolite was lethal by itself, and in combination with amonible and tremolite fibers were real killers indeed. The WCO doctor and the WCO conspired to deny the claim, the same thing the government did in denying responsibility for the asbestos in the Biscayne Annex. I was not allowed to sue the government, remember. That is why the Congress set up the FECA to divert lawsuits to the WCO who in turn denied the claims. This then is their form of benevolent insurance. It's a joke. The WCO denies all claims when they can do so with impunity, using adversarial means, which they are forbidden by the Act itself, to use. Even when their guilt was palpable and irrevocable, they still arrogantly denied claims. And even if they lost they refused to pay the winning lawyer's fee.

I referred them back to my two experts and the fact that Biscayne Annex had been closed because this was the kind of asbestos that could kill the employees.

They again denied the claim. I can tell you I was devastated.

My asbestos attorney told me to write them that we were hearing depositions in the trial of the installers who had installed the asbestos. I was to tell them to keep the claim open until it was proved in the deposition phase that the asbestos in the Biscayne Annex was the same asbestos that was found in John's lungs. I wrote them such a request on July 5, 1995.

They never sent me any response to let me know if the case was still being held open to officially establish the date of the last turn down which would become exceedingly important down the line. The last form letter of action was sent in June of 1994. They did not send me any response after July 1995 telling me that they would keep the case open, or that I had the right to take the case on appeal to the Employees' Compensation Arbitration Board. So I was waiting for their final turn down of my request to keep the case open.

I wrote to the president of the United States about it. I wrote to the first lady. They both referred me to the Justice Department. The federal attorney I talked to in Janet Reno's office advised me to request a hearing in front of the ECAB, the Employees Compensation Arbitration Board, the highest authority in Federal Workmen's Compensation Claims. I told him I had asked for the case to remain open since new evidence would be coming out in the deposition for the trial, but that I had not heard one way or the other from the WCO.

It was one year later in the summer of 1996 that I hired an attorney to file for an appeal in front of the ECAB and had him contact the WCO with my permission to get my husband's complete file. The WCO refused to send it to him. It took me a whole month of going back and forth with them trying to get the file that held up my filing for a hearing in front of the ECAB until August of 1996. By the time we got the file we were beyond the one-year limit for filing before the board. It was in no way our fault. We needed the file to verify the letters and documentation I had sent to the WCO. They purposely did not send the file until they knew we would be untimely in our petition. They also sent, illegally, a letter to the board, who were supposed to be kept unbiased, stating that their last turn down had been on July 5, 1995, which also made our appeal untimely by one month. IT WAS NOT A LETTER FROM THEM WITH THE DATE OF THE TURN DOWN BUT MY LETTER TO

THEM ASKING THEM TO KEEP THE CASE OPEN THAT THEY USED TO BIAS THE BOARD. In other words they misrepresented to the board that that date was their date of turn down when it wasn't. They had never sent me a response to my letter of that date as to whether they would keep the date open as requested, or close it which would have been their official date of turn down and would have come after our August appeal and would have made us timely in our appeal before the board. THEY NEVER SENT ME SUCH A LETTER WITH A DATE OF TURN DOWN. That answer would have established the official date of the last turn down to meet the requirements of the board who needed that knowledge to determine if we were timely or not.

Since the WCO had failed to send me a responding official letter in answer to my request, they falsely used the date of my request as the date of their turn down. I called the board's secretary and told her the WCO had refused to forward the file in a timely manner, and that we could not fill in the box truthfully for the office's last turn down date since they never officially answered that request. That secretary was hostile, rude and obnoxious. She never forwarded my explanation to the board of why we were untimely, by one month, because the WCO had held the file to make us untimely, and that they were lying when they used the date of my letter as their last turn down date, that they had never sent me an official letter with the date of the turn down, and therefore we were truthful in telling the board we did not know the date of the last turn down and could not fill that box in truthfully.

As my representative, my lawyer wrote a letter to the ECAB notifying them that he was my lawyer. He told them he was willing to come to Washington, D.C. to speak in front of the board. He asked that a form be sent to file for appeal. They sent the form and said they would put us on the docket. Their secretary was again hostile and rude, but we got the forms.

We filled the form but, again, we could not fill in the one box that asked for the date of the last turn down since we had no date officially from the Compensation office. The secretary of the board told me, in a "catch 22" I had to fill in a date. I told her we didn't know the date because the WCO had never told us officially that they had turned down my request to keep the case open. She would not tell my attorney what to do in that situation. We asked her to inform the board of why we were untimely. She refused. She kept sending us letters telling us the board had to have the date and I kept telling her we didn't have the date to ask the WCO. In the end we kept the box open with an explanation.

The WCO, who were not supposed to influence this board either way, sent that letter lying by saying the turn down date was July, 1995, which it wasn't, the date would have been their response letter telling us the case was being held open and that date would have made us timely before the board. The secretary to the board, without ever bringing the case before the board, called my attorney and asked him what date of turn down was I using. She said that box had to be filled in <u>truthfully</u> on the form for appeal. When I told her I had been turned down officially two times, twice formally by mail, but my last request to keep the case open had gone unanswered by the WCO. She would not tell me which date was proper to note and which date was the accurate one to be put on the appeal form. However, we were on the docket for the next month. My attorney and I were happy as kids out of school even if it meant going to Washington, D.C. to be heard.

And here is the most unbelievable happening of all. THE BOARD DISMISSED THE CASE BECAUSE WE DID NOT FILL IN

THAT DATE BOX, AND BECAUSE WE WERE UNTIMELY BY ONE MONTH!

They did not dismiss on the merits of the case, or the material evidence in the case, they dismissed because their arrogant secretary would not tell them the WCO had made us untimely by not sending the file when requested, and by not issuing an official letter to me with a turn down date for my last request to keep the case open that I had sent on July 5, 1995. Therefore, we should be heard because none of that was our fault but lay with the WCO and the WCO had lied about the date. After eight years of fighting every step of the way to keep the claim open, and following the rules, we had been turned down with dismissal papers. The three board members all signed off on the dismissal never knowing what the case was about, why we were late and why we couldn't fill in the date they wanted that wasn't even material to the body of our appeal. They just didn't care. It was all a conspiracy between the Board, the Government, and the WCO to never allow an appellant their day in court.

They said denial was because the claim for appeal was one month late. The board never heard our explanation that the WCO made us one month late by holding up the file. Their secretary told us we could not appeal their decision, that it was final.

It was a conspiracy. The board did not do their job by reading the case and asking questions of their secretary as to why she didn't tell them why we could not comply with their request. They should also have disciplined the WCO for writing a letter to them to try and bias them against our case or that they had lied about the date of turn down, or they had made us late by not sending us the file in a timely manner. Once it was on the docket it should have been heard and decided on the merits face to face with me and my lawyer not on the fact the WCO had never given us a date of response to use. These people helped to bury John a little deeper in his grave and they should all be ashamed.

They robbed John of his day in court because of a lie told by the WCO of the turn down date, and the refusal to forward the file that was legally mine, and do it in a timely manner.

In the appeals board dismissing the case there was no avenue for grievance or appeal that we were ever told about.

Because of one date, not even important to the material questions in the case, just a housekeeping question, and because of the lies of the WCO and the secretary's inappropriate malice, John's rights to due process under the Constitution were denied. An insignificant date and the WCO refusal to send John's file promptly had cost us our chance before the board due to their incompetence not ours. We did what was asked of us, to tell the truth, and they did not want to hear the truth. They wrongfully dismissed our case on the say-so of an arrogant clerk and the lies of the WCO. I so charge them, let them speak if they dare.

Is it any wonder attorneys do not want to get mixed up with the WCO or the appeals board?

They do not go by due process rules of evidence. They go by their own rules. They keep changing opinions so they can deny claims. And the appeals board is all intertwined with the very program they are charged to police. Isn't it blatant, arrogant and heinous?

From beginning to end, not one person in that office gave me help, assistance or the time of day. You may wonder why nearly a year passed between John's death and my first claim to the WCO. That's because of John's union. That story is told in the next chapter.

CHAPTER TEN
THE GOOD OLD UNION

John was a staunch union man. He had first belonged to the Teamster's Union in Cleveland, Ohio. From the day he went to work for the Post Office, he remained a member in good standing of the Postal Workers Union and was in the process of joining the Supervisors' union just before he died. He always told me, "If you ever have any trouble with the Post Office to get in touch with the union."

The denial of my wrongful death claim by the WCO had me hunting around for a lawyer who could fight this issue and not charge a high fee. I figured with more than a million dollars at stake, I would be able to find a lawyer willing to take the case on contingency—meaning the lawyer would not make any money unless I got my money and then a 60-40 division in my favor.

I called all over town for such a lawyer and found none who would take a case involving the WCO. They called it a crooked program and that it would refuse to pay out benefits, even if you had irrefutable proof. They would make a member go to the courts, a very expensive and long process, rather than pay out benefits. You have to remember I was under a time limit of one year set by the WCO in asking for an appeal hearing before the ECAB after my final turn down from the program, which they never officially sent me.

I vividly remember the day when my foggy brain seemed to clear and it popped into my head that I should not be the one running around trying to find help. John was a member in good standing with the Postal Workers Union. There were certain benefits they provided to members and their survivors. One of these obligations was to provide a lawyer to a member or survivor who was having a problem with a claim filed with the WCO. I know this because I was a union president once. We provided such legal representation to members. I called the union hall the same day.

I immediately talked with a woman who was Director of Claims. She worked for the American Postal Workers Union at 7910 N.W. 25th Street, Suite 200, Miami, Florida.

She was a friendly woman who listened politely to my complaint. At the end she said the union did indeed take cases like mine. As director of the claims department, she would read a copy of the initial claim I had sent to WCO. Along with that initial form, I should send along the hospital records and the letter from the surgeon verifying that

John was not a cigarette smoker, and depositions from the Mt. Sinai Hospital. She acknowledged readily that the Biscayne Annex had been shut down because of the asbestos scandal and told me I had a very good case to get death benefits. I was to leave everything in her hands. She would handle the case from there. She also said, if we had to go to a hearing the union attorney would represent me.

You cannot imagine the joy I felt.

I immediately sent her all the records she asked for including depositions by the Mt. Sinai doctors along with the letter from the surgeon thinking this would be a long process. By then, due to the time restrictions on lawsuits, I had hired the asbestos lawyer, and I was busy supplying information to him, giving my deposition to the five asbestos companies who had installed the asbestos in the Biscayne Annex. I was also employed full-time.

After a month went by, I called the Claims Director. She told me the union was getting the appeal together to fight the WCO doctor's first and second opinions and assured me there was movement in the case. I was completely satisfied with her assurances and told her I would not bother her again. I would wait for her to contact me.

What the union should have been doing, and what I believed they were doing, was contacting the WCO to let them know they were now my representative and that all correspondence should go to them. They would have sent notice that they were challenging the opinions of the WCO doctor. First for being in error in his opinion that John's cancer was caused by cigarette smoking. This had been countered with the surgeon's letter, and in his second invalid opinion that the asbestos in the Biscayne Annex was not lethal. They would have cited the shutting down of the Biscayne Annex by the government as proof the asbestos was dangerous and that it was through their negligence in installing it that caused John to be exposed and finally deceased because of this negligence.

They would also notify the WCO that if they denied the claim again they would represent me at a hearing in Jacksonville. If, after that hearing, if the claim was still denied they would travel to Washington, D.C. to represent me in front of the ECAB for an appeal. That's what the director told me they were doing. In my faith that the union had everything under control I felt I no longer had to contact the WCO. However, being the persistent kind, I kept writing letters asking that the case remain active for new evidence.

During the following months, I was contacted again and again by the Union Claims Director telling me the strategy the union was going to use. She told me just enough month by month that I felt the case was an ongoing reality.

Then one day, toward the end of the year, I called the union. To my everlasting surprise I was told the Claims Director was no longer working for the union! I pressed the representative for information about John's case. She told me I had to talk either to the union lawyer or the union president. I opted for the union president. I got the president on the phone and I could tell something was not right because the Union President was immediately hostile and rude. I recognized that hostility from the hospital, the surgeon, from the WCO and the ECBA. What hurt most, was this is someone who knew John well and was supposed to be a friend. The President should have been enthusiastic to see that John's death was given the proper respect it deserved.

The President verified that the Claims Director no longer worked there and said my case had never been worked on. No notices had been sent to the WCO, no records forwarded, no letter from the surgeon received. At no time did the union lawyer write to say they represented me. The President tried to convince me it was all the Claims Director's fault, but I said because the Claims Director was no longer there, it was still the union's obligation to represent the case. I said I had been waiting for almost a year for action thinking the union was handling the procedure. I explained that my time limit would not be met. The WCO had never been contacted in any way, the President said. It was not the union's obligation to supply a lawyer. I responded that the union's representative had cost me precious time. I wanted to talk to a union lawyer. The President refused. In a most hostile manner, I was told to go join a class action suit against the asbestos companies.

I said this claim was against the WCO and had nothing to do with class action suits. It was the union's responsibility to provide a legal representative when a member's survivor was having problems with a death benefit claim. That was why members paid dues.

The President once again denied the union had any responsibility, never apologized for the union's mishandling of the case, and hung up on me.

I tried several times to get to speak to a union attorney, but it was quite obvious, at least to me, that the President had alerted the receptionist not to put my calls through.

It made me think the union was in bed with the government regarding the asbestos mess. They had effectively put a lid on the condemnation of the building and moving the employees in a hush-hush operation. They also wanted to keep the union members from filing claims to blow the operation sky high, and I have no doubt they told the union officials what to tell members who came to the union needing legal help. That is my opinion and I am sticking to it. There was very little about the closing and condemnation of the Biscayne Annex in the papers, so they were doing damage control that could have extended to the union leadership. They were afraid the whole thing would blow wide open, and every employee and member of the public, who had worked or visited that death trap building, would be filing negligence claims against the government, which they had every right to do. I don't know if money exchanged hands, or if threats were made, I only know the union officials refused to fulfill their obligations as advocates for the members and discouraged any contact with those who had legitimate asbestos claims.

I believe they refused to help John's co-worker in her claim for asbestos-related lung cancer and did not bring the union's power to bear on the Post Office officials, the government, or the WCO on her behalf. It probably was that WCO doctor or some weasel just like him, who denied her claim because she was a smoker. They should have had her lungs tested for asbestos—it was the government's responsibility to do so. They pretended that no member of the union died of asbestos-related cancer from exposure to the asbestos in the Biscayne Annex, now that the cancers were finally showing up after twenty years. (Which the medical field certified would be the length of time for them to manifest.)

They did not utter one objection when they found out the government had admitted negligence by condemning the Annex or against the fact they did not x-ray John. As far as I know, the union never made any protest about the dangers of that lethal environment and never represented any member or their survivors against the WCO or the ECAB. These were the only two places federal employees could sue for death benefits caused by the workplace, as the union was pledged to do.

Such a conspiracy would be unforgivable, a cold fraud perpetrated on the membership if true. I should have sued them then for the time and money they cost me and for the fraud they had perpetrated on me. They knew their representative had taken my case but they never informed me in that whole year that they had done nothing with the case.

I truly believe the Claims Director was doing proper duty and that the union punished the Director for doing her duty to protect a member's survivor. Wherever you are Claims Director, I hope you read this and understand I have no animosity toward you.

Though the union had no hand in building the Annex and did not share the negligence of the government that killed John, they could be responsible, as co-conspirators. They killed John by not championing his rights to receive compensation from the WCO, and, if true, for assigning their allegiance to the Post Office who stymied any mention of the asbestos scandal.

I was also told by another attorney that I could not sue the union unless I could prove conspiracy between the officers and the government. Of course I had no smoking gun and would never be able to make the case. But, these individuals know who they are and how they were involved in their betrayal of John and his family.

They never told the newspapers or the press that it was bad for the government to have exposed workers at the Biscayne Annex, their union members, to asbestosis and lung cancer. They never fought to get their members' rightful claims approved. They never said how sad it was that John died from asbestos lung cancer, and they all knew him very well.

Never, by word or deed, did they stand up for their fallen member who was in their ranks for 23 years and their friend.

They never went on strike to protect the members from the denial of claims by the WCO or the ECAB members.

"Vengeance is mine," says the Lord.

So be it.

CHAPTER ELEVEN
THE ASBESTOS LAWYER

After approximately eighteen months of piddling around, first with the WCO then with the union, thinking the Workmen's Compensation Death Benefit was sufficient to last the rest of my life I was now forced to scramble for a lawyer who would take our case at the last minute. I was referred to an expert asbestos lawyer whom I shall call Sydney.

What can I say about Sydney, our asbestos lawyer? He was charming, slick and sometimes sly. He was a handsome man, slender and tall. Sam's lawyer friend gave us a helping hand with this referral. He put us in contact with Sydney because he said Sydney was the "best asbestos lawyer" in the area. By this time the two-year statute of limitations on lawsuits under the state law, loomed large. Only a few months of grace remained.

Both my sons were devastated with the way they had lost their father. Sam had devoted his life to helping people addicted to drugs and alcohol. He served as the Director of Treatment in a rehab facility. John, our youngest son, had followed his father into the Post Office and remains a supervisor there today. My sons were with me every step of the way, offering encouragement and support. All three of us understood that there were only two ways to derive justice: by public apology from those who had contributed to John's murder, or an enormous monetary penalty that would warn them never to do this to another human being.

Of course, no one was going to take responsibility for their negligence without a fight, so we opted for the jury trial where all facts would be made public. I can tell you money was a secondary issue, even though the government had robbed me of John's earning power and left me without this source of income when he had many years of productivity ahead of him.

All my family ever wanted was justice and an acknowledgement that the government's negligence had caused John's death. We could not sue the government under the Federal Employees Compensation Act, though every other citizen in the United States is entitled to due process under the law. We had not received John's death benefit from the WCO and we had gotten no help from the union. So, what was left to us?

What was left was a public trial, with all the attendant publicity and media coverage that option would entail. It was worth it to be before a jury of our peers. The Constitution guarantees due process to all citizens, and guarantees a trial by jury. Only a bad judge accepts a move for Summary Judgment in lieu of a jury trial. On the day we went to meet Sydney, the importance of our last avenue of grievance weighed heavily on our minds.

Sam, John and I sat with Sydney while he explained to us what he intended to do. He was going to sue the two big companies responsible for installing the asbestos in the Biscayne Annex. Along with them, there were a handful of smaller companies that helped. They were included in our suit.

I mentioned the WCO but Sydney said, too, that no lawyer was willing to get involved in a case against a government agency well known for denying claims for any reason. He said it was not within his legal expertise. We would have to pursue that avenue ourselves.

He also agreed that suing the union would be an exercise in futility, unless we had hard evidence they were not willing to legally represent John because they had made a deal with the Post Office officials. If I could prove money passed hands or the union officials had been coerced in any way, then, and only then, could we pursue a suit against the union officials.

Sydney also felt the hospital and doctors might have been the targets of a suit. Again, it would be difficult to establish exactly what happened to send John into shock. Of course we had no way in the world to prove any of this stuff beyond our gut feelings that such was the case, along with the hostile treatment we had received, common sense and records of John's blood. The only avenue open to us was to sue the installers of the asbestos.

As an extension of this agreement, Sydney gave me a contingency agreement to sign. He said it was a <u>standard</u> <u>contingency</u> agreement. I had been involved in a small accident years before in which an attorney had me sign a <u>standard</u> <u>contingency</u> agreement. I received sixty percent of the small settlement; forty percent went to the attorney. That was the end of it.

So when Sydney told me we were signing a standard contingency agreement that's what "agreement" and "contingency" meant to me. I'm sure Sydney was not a mind reader and had no idea how I viewed the words. He told us he would get forty percent unless he had to go to trial and then his take would be fifty percent because he would have more preparation to do. If all the companies settled to our satisfaction, there would be no need for a trial or appeal, so he would try for a fair settlement first. His one worry was that we were not going to be ready in time to meet the two-year statute of limitations. Sydney decided to file the case in federal court since it involved the government and the installers putting asbestos in the Biscayne Annex where they knew it was dangerous, according to popular knowledge at the time. By then there had been many articles and much research done on the lethal substance, starting in the 1800s, that pinpointed asbestos as a carcinogen agent and the proven cause of lung cancer and asbestosis. In 1953, when the Annex had been plastered with it, the companies would have known of the dangerous properties and what the popular thinking about it was, expressed by experts in the field of medicine and in the views of their fellow insulators. They had only to contact the Library of Congress to find out. John had been exposed for twelve and one half years at the Annex. It had taken twenty-three years for the lung cancer and asbestosis to make its appearance.

At this point I told Sydney that John could have been exposed in 1964 at a Christmas party he attended at the Annex. My husband's official date of employment, according to his personnel records, was in June of 1964. He thought that was interesting, but I don't remember what he said about it. I do know my attorney was more worried about filing before the two-year deadline expired. He might not have understood the importance of that information. He may have thought it played no role in the case at all.

And so Sydney filed our case right under the wire with only a few days to spare. I can't be sure of that date but I know we cut it extremely close.

Among the companies named in the suit were the two large ones: along with several smaller companies.

The first thing Sydney did was get depositions from John's co-workers, especially John's friend who had worked side by side with John. She was the one who also had a lung removed. They all cooperated and came in and gave testimony. Then Sydney dispatched an assistant to New York to Mt. Sinai Hospital with the tissue samples from John's lungs. The pathologist from the original hospital had said there were no asbestos fibers in John's lungs. The electronic microscope and Energy Dispersion Spectocopy at Mt. Sinai found his lungs full of fibers of a very lethal form of asbestos—comprised of chrysotile, amonibole and tremolite fibers. It proved that the asbestos in Biscayne Annex was the friable type. It also proved that John had breathed in very dangerous fibers every minute of the day and night on his assigned shift. So had his co-worker along with all the employees and the public who entered that building.

At this time the whole country knew about asbestos. Big awards in the millions of dollars were being awarded in private cases. A great many class actions suits were brought by shipyard workers who had been exposed as early as 1941, the beginning of World War II.

At the same time, Agent Orange cases were being filed. This extremely lethal and dangerous substance is similar in its effects to asbestos, causing slow-growing cancer. The New York legislature and courts had the good sense to recognize that these materials caused a slow growing type of injury and struck down any time limit to liability for the producers and manufacturers of Agent Orange. The Florida legislature had done the same thing by removing the statute of repose from the Florida law that set a time limit for the manufacturers and users liability. The Supreme Court of Florida, under the pressure of the products' manufacturers, reinstated the statute. However, they did not set up a separate method by which asbestos cases could come to the courts without a time limit on the appearance of their plaintiff's cancers. They co-mingled this slow-growing cancer with observable and minor injuries caused by manufactured products. They had no business overriding the legislature. Here again, I feel, it was a deal, plain and simple, with asbestos murderers who did not want the courts to set up any law in the cases of injury by asbestos.

I was called very early to face the companies we were suing. Their representatives sat around the table during my deposition taking turns asking questions. I wasn't nervous or intimidated. In fact, I was thrilled. At last I was given a chance to give testimony in an official courtroom setting, with a court reporter recording everything I said <u>verbatim</u>.

If this had been the case with the WCO'S doctor he would not have been allowed to render two decisions after we disproved his first opinion. He would have been stuck with his testimony and I would have gotten my husband's death benefits.

Actually, each lawyer and representative of the insurance companies was courteous and polite. There were very few questions they labeled unresponsive. In about three hours the ordeal was over.

In the meantime, the federal court had ruled we were timely with our lawsuit. We could ask to be put on the docket of the Federal District Judge.

Sydney was in intense negotiations with the companies. The three smaller companies opted out of the suit with a settlement of $20,000. My sons and I were overjoyed. I had made it my intention of sharing the monies with my sons. It wouldn't give them back their father, but it would give them the feeling that someone was taking responsibility for murdering John through their negligence. I felt the $4,000 apiece we would receive would in some way be a symbol of the rightness of our cause.

Then a letter from Sydney dampened hopes that things were turning our way. Sydney was keeping the full check to pay for his out-of-pocket expenses for the trial. What? That couldn't be right. "Contingency" meant he got 40% to our 60%. He was taking 100%. He should have paid for his office expenses out of his own pocket as the cost of doing business in the case. I looked at the long list of charges he sent me with the letter and burst into tears.

I admired Sydney as our champion. Anything he had advised me to do, down to giving interviews to the legal press to explain our case, I did. I had watched him with admiration as he filed the case and won our right to go to court. I had seen activity and official actions for the first time in the case. He had comforted me, been kind to my sons and had been very straightforward in his explanations. I knew how contingency agreements were supposed to work and it wasn't in this manner. I was more bewildered than angry, more hurt than outraged. Not long before I had read of a man who faced this exact same situation. He had gotten nothing from his settlement; his lawyer kept it all. It had been filed with the ethics committee of the American Bar Association. That lawyer had been reprimanded and had to pay back a goodly percentage of his ill-gotten gains.

I was sick of lawyers, sick of repeating my pleas for justice in many different venues, sick of the doctor of the WCO, sick of union lawyers who gave no help, sick of dealing with lying and deceitful people. And now I was face to face with another setback, facing more legal questions. The one I trusted the most seemed to be showing signs of a darker side. I decided before I took any action to talk sensibly to Sydney.

I called him. He explained in his charming way that these monies were not going into his pocket. He was getting ready for trial and it was expensive. He gave me his litany of charges. A New York trip, the depositions from the New York doctors, the depositions of John's co-workers, court costs, stenographic costs, copies, telephone—the tale went on and on. He ended up with his all-American speech. I thought he should have a flag to wave.

"We're going to trial for millions of dollars," he explained. "Do you want to jeopardize your chances to get these people who did this to John? This is an investment in that process, otherwise you couldn't afford it. And if we have to appeal it will cost even more. The odds and the mood of the country are in our favor for a huge award. We are going to get these guys. Our chances are more than fifty-fifty that we will win. Would I cheat you? I'm using all my expertise. I've had millions of dollars awarded in cases before. It's a good case. You're my star witness. We're going to make them sorry they ever heard of asbestos, much less use it in a government building. And what about John? Doesn't he deserve his day in court?"

If these were not his exact words, it was the essence of Sydney's reasons for keeping the money. I can't tell you how disappointed I was. Not for the money. We never counted on the money. My hero had clay feet but what he said made sense. However, he was the only way to justice left to us and in the end I relented.

The boys wanted me to go to the Bar Association but I found myself regurgitating the same line Sydney had fed me. We were going to trial. It was expensive. We were highly favored to win. The mood of the country was to give us our day in court. After we talked it over I called Sydney again. I told him I didn't want to go for millions in court. We only wanted the amount of money John would have earned had he lived and worked until retirement. Anything above that won in a settlement Sydney could keep. He promised any other settlement from the big companies would be as stated in the contingency agreement, 60-40 or 50-50 if a trial or an appeal were necessary.

And so we let him keep twenty thousand dollars.

Suddenly one of the big companies settled privately for $10,000 plus the interest on that amount of money over a one or two year waiting period, so we wouldn't get it right away. After the allotted time, we each received almost $3,000. In a class action suit against this company some participants were paid nearly a million dollars. I protested to Sydney and asked why he had settled for so little from this company. Had we joined the class action suit, we stood to receive an enormous settlement. Sydney said at the time, before the class action suit, that he settled for what he thought we could get from this company, though they were insured for millions of dollars. He said he didn't know about the class action suit when he settled. As for the $3,000, we looked upon it as a satisfaction that someone had finally taken responsibility for John's death, even if under threat of court action. Privately, I thought this company had done the right thing, though they gave meager compensation. That meager $3,000 gave me some closure to this whole nightmare and some satisfaction.

Sydney made a point of telling me he had made a special concession in that settlement. He took only 25% instead of the 40% he was entitled to. I thanked him profusely for his goodness and his kindness; I think even writing a letter to him to that effect. A long time later I found out that the court in the settlement had capped the lawyer's fees at 25%. That amount was what Sydney was ordered to take by the courts instead of the 40%. So all of his blarney was not true. But that was Sydney.

There was only one company left—the big company. Sydney said that's what we had to concentrate on now. This was the big one. This was the one that would pay for their murderous ways standing in for the government. This was the one that counted.

In September our case against them was placed on the Federal Judge's court docket for a trial that was scheduled to take place in only a month or a few weeks.

My boys and I were excited. We finally saw light at the end of the tunnel. I had researched this Judge a little and knew he was considered a liberal, fair-minded jurist, just the man whose many rulings showed him to be a humanitarian with a large heart for the common man. He believed deeply in the Constitution, in the right to due process, and in a trial by jury on the material facts.

Life was good. In a few weeks we would have a decision from a jury panel of our peers who had been found impartial and qualified to sit as our judges.

For the first time I felt the time was near when I could close this chapter of my life with a happy ending of justice for John. That's all I asked for, justice for my John.

CHAPTER TWELVE
OF THE CONGRESS, BY THE
CONGRESS AND FOR THE CONGRESS

Would you think that the Congress of the United States would be able to reach into the legal system and interfere with cases waiting to go to trial? In our free country, under a Constitution that guarantees due process, the branches are separate and distinct. Above all, they are separate with their own independent responsibilities and procedures. The legislative body, the Congress, is forbidden to interfere in any way with the judicial branch, just as the judicial branch is forbidden to affect the enactment of laws. Of course, the executive branch cannot make laws or decide legal cases anymore than Congress can circumvent the legal system and act as judge in a legal proceeding.

Ideology that drives a political party is also what drives political decisions, along with the promise of re-election. Millions of dollars from special interests groups are donated to keep their man in office. Of course there is a price tag with these financial windfalls, and that is a favorable vote when the special interest company's interests are at stake.

The ideology of the Republican Party (they cannot deny it) is to protect big business at any cost. They are the party of the wealthy. Believe me, if it were the Democrats who had perpetrated this bit of chicanery I would be on top of them too. But it is the Republicans that protect the huge industrial complex and the wealthy corporations with their mantra for tax cuts, and their actions against environmental laws. In return, these huge donors send millions of dollars to the coffers of the Republican Party. In return, Republicans protect them from having to pay out large settlements to the common man for injury or death caused by their products or lack of safety procedures.

At the time we were awaiting trial in Miami, the Republican politicians were secretly busy in Washington formulating a plan whereby the asbestos industry would be saved from ruin. They were creating a method of short-circuiting thousands of lawsuits filed as class action suits by shipyard workers and any other huge group of people who had been exposed to the killing properties of asbestos. There had already been judgments from juries all around the country, in single wrongful death cases, that totaled millions of dollars in death benefits and punitive damages against these large companies who were donators and friends of the Republican politicians. My case was not part of a class action suit. It was a private lawsuit legally awaiting trial in Miami.

I learned later from a justice department deputy that there had been a meeting (he sent me the minutes but they are now lost) that included two very high-ranking Republicans, one in the judiciary and one in the executive branches. It was a little-advertised meeting to discuss legislation to help their hapless friends in the asbestos industry who donated monies to the Republican Party to protect them from legally filed lawsuits. These special interests were calling in a favor. In other words, these men were circumventing the due process clause of the Constitution to illegally keep their cronies from losing their shirts in court and they were using politics to do it.

What right had any governmental official to interfere with these cases by trying to stop their trip through the court system? Wasn't that a conflict of interests since this high-ranking official might have to hear appeals from the aggrieved litigants at a future date? And why would he be mixed up in drawing up legislation? Wasn't that a power only of the Congress? Take my word for it, he shouldn't be, but he was.

Further, what right had the other Republican high-ranking official to stick his nose into judicial matters and procedures by using the executive branch's powers to protect asbestos manufacturers from legitimately filed lawsuits? And he did it blatantly with political chicanery, using his powerful office to force his allies in Congress to pass legislation they had not initiated.

This is the kind of political corruption that results from untold dollars donated by wealthy entities, when the little guy has none to give and subsequently no power. It is the huge amounts of money given to members of Congress and to the central parties that corrupt everyone and give special-interest groups with these large amounts of money the clout to get Congress to circumvent the Constitution and the legal system, to turn it on its head.

At the cited meeting, legislation called the "Multi-Districting Bill" was born. This legislation had as its sole purpose to take all legitimately filed asbestos cases against the asbestos manufacturers out of the federal courts and move all of those cases to a single Judge's court in Philadelphia for settlement. Have you ever heard of such a thing? I can only believe that that Judge was a Republican, too. I believe he was told to sit on these cases. Instead of being heard by a jury who could award any amount of money and impose punitive damages, they would now be heard by one judge who would demand that lawyers settle their clients' cases for next to nothing. There were orchestrated speeches saying the trial lawyers were clogging the courts with cases. You should remember that. It was a disgrace and a ruse that robbed every victim or survivor of their constitutional right to have their cases heard by a jury of their peers.

The rationalization of Congress and what they blamed for passing this sleazy scam was that the number of asbestos cases filed were "clogging the court system." To move them all to one judge in Philadelphia would speed up settlements. You tell me how taking these cases from 80 judges across the country and moving to one judge would speed up the process? I can tell you, it didn't.

Congress never did address the question of constitutionality. I assume that was why the high ranking personage was included to give a blanket opinion that it was okay, thereby removing the legitimate recourse of the victims to appeal to the Supreme Court.

Congress passed the legislation. Both parties joined in to protect their benefactors who were the hens that laid the golden eggs for their re-election.

Under this legislation every case scheduled for trial by jury was grabbed illegally from their federal judge and dragged kicking and screaming to the all-knowing, all-powerful magistrate, the Judge of Philadelphia.

I remember that our Miami Federal Judge, bless his heart, said that his court was not so burdened that he could not hear these cases. It would do little good to show there was a scam going on. The law was the law and all cases were moved. Our case was to be heard in just two days when it was stolen from our Federal Judge's court and sent to Philadelphia. I have to give Sydney credit. We tried to re-file in state court but to no avail.

And so the Congress of the United States hammered another indignity into John's coffin.

The Bible says government is supposed to protect widows and orphans. I'm sure God never envisioned the crooks in our Congress or he wouldn't have laid out that lofty expectation.

My case perished in the Philadelphia Judge's court, smothered by three years of inaction! Speedy settlement? What a joke. I again wrote letters to the president, to the justice department, to my representatives in

Congress. The answers from them were always the same: "Nothing can be done."

I wrote and called the Philadelphia Judge's office many, many times to find out the progress of the case. Sydney's attitude was one of complete resignation. No amount of citizen action could get the case remanded back to Miami. In the beginning we tried to get the media interested in this illegal miscarriage of justice. Only the attorney's newspaper published an article, and this from the legal point of view.

I don't remember lawyers raising the question of constitutionality or the subversion of "due process." In any settlement they would still receive their fees. No one went running to the Supreme Court for redress. My complaint to Sydney and the Philadelphia Judge's clerk that my case was not part of a class action suit but a private, wrongful death case got no response. I was upset with Sydney for not keeping a running complaint going with the court in Philadelphia or for not bringing up the fact that ours was a private case entitled to due process. Sydney's attitude of benign acceptance dampened my fighting spirit. However, it did not stop me from maintaining a barrage of objections to the clerk and to any other official I could think of.

My case lay dormant for three years. The explanation by Congress that this procedure would "hasten settlement" was a lie. Everyone knew it. My case would have been settled in a couple of weeks had it been allowed to proceed in Miami's Federal Judge's court. Instead it languished for three years.

Now I ask: Don't you think three years would have given Sydney time to anticipate our opponents every step of action in every contingency? Discovery had been completed. Both sides had given depositions. Technical information had been exchanged. There were material questions that were stipulated by Sydney that I thought should never have been stipulated to. All material facts were still being argued over. With Sydney's expertise in asbestos law he should have anticipated every legal remedy the opposition could take advantage of and been prepared for any contingency, no matter what strategy they might come up with. It was his responsibility to give us his best advice at all times.

Many days I called Sydney to ask if he had been in contact with Philadelphia. He said he had initiated several calls but nothing was happening.

Then one day he called and told me the clerk had called for a conference call with

Sydney. I can't be sure how long after the initial kidnapping of the case this took place, but my gut feeling tells me it was past the two-year mark. Sydney reported they refused to remand back the case and no settlement was forthcoming. But he told me in an upbeat way when it did come back he was ready. "We have a good chance of winning."

Three years dragged by. I had written so many letters and made so many phone calls I knew the clerk by name. I was probably listed in Washington, D.C. as a crackpot and a troublemaker. I berated my Florida congressmen and senators for their inaction. Their standard mantra was: "It's in the courts. We can't do anything." My response was always: "If you legislators hadn't passed this legislation illegally it wouldn't be in the system in Philadelphia and I would have had John's day in court a long time ago." You can see I didn't make any friends.

Then after a long period adrift, feeling my cries for justice were unheard by God, He answered my prayers. Sydney called and told me the case had been remanded back to Miami. I can truthfully say it was all solely through my efforts and campaigning. My refusal to accept any settlement convinced the Philadelphia court of the futility of keeping it any longer. For a case hijacked with promises of quick settlement, to languish for three years shows how shameful the scheme was in the first place. It was a sham from beginning to end to buy time. Thousands of unsettled asbestos cases, private and class action are still out there in the American court system awaiting settlement.

This is what my ordeal taught me. Any Republican who had any official role to play in the handling of my case would want to see it fail and would be biased in favor of the asbestos manufacturers and against awarding any compensation or punitive damages to us through a jury if they could find any way to avoid it. That was the Republican mindset. Don't think for a minute that judges are not affected by their ideology and biases, especially Republican judges who wish to advance to the appellate court from the circuit court.

The court in Philadelphia remanded the case back to Miami and ordered it to be returned to the Miami Federal Judge's docket. And here is the last nail in John's coffin. It was not sent back to our Miami Judge's docket, it was sent to the district court where it did not belong to another judge who, I think, was a Republican-friendly Judge who would see to it that the case never saw a jury. Get it? It was not sent to the Federal Court or to the friend of the common man, instead it was sent to the district court where it did not belong and to a judge who read the law very narrowly. Sydney never challenged this erroneous assignment.

CHAPTER THIRTEEN
MEDIATION A DISASTER

The atmosphere at this time in The Capitol and in the courts was a growing battle between Republicans and trial lawyers. The Republicans strongly objected to what they termed "frivolous lawsuits"—lawyers clogging up the court system. Their intention, where product liability cases were concerned, was to put a cap of $100,000 on awards by juries for damages and punitive punishments. I have to agree with some of their reasoning. We had become a litigious country, filing lawsuits over spurious claims and winning huge awards. Trial lawyers, too, often used poor judgment in the defense of spurious cases looking for easy money. However, such a cap on benefits would not be enough to take care of a client, for instance, who had been the victim of malpractice by a doctor, and whose negligence left that person disabled or in a coma for life, or products that killed, such as asbestos.

War between Republican ideology and the incompetence and greed of some trial lawyers grew hot. Thus, the Multi-Districting legislation had been born, forcing premature settlements on victims and their families by sitting on their cases in the courts. This delaying tactic left thousands of cases in the courts. This mission by the Republicans to get rid of asbestos cases, among other types of product liability cases, seeped down to Republican-ruled state legislatures and to Republican judges. A distinct party line surfaced. The line was if you were a good little judge you would do away with expensive asbestos cases from the court system. The other part of that line was that if you were a good little judge perhaps down the line you would be promoted. All you had to do was read the law narrowly, dismiss the cases, and everyone was home free. These narrow rulings would also bar access to the courts by limiting the body of asbestos law and putting unreasonably short time limits on manufacturers' liabilities. These time limits did not allow for the reality that it took a lot longer than twelve years for asbestos cancer to show itself. The Supreme Court of Florida had ignored this well documented reality and overruled the legislature by putting a twelve-year time limit on all Product Liability cases. It was and is a nonsensical ruling in Florida and one made for political reasons. That is my opinion.

When my case was remanded back to Miami it should have been returned to the judge's court from which it had been taken.

But Philadelphia couldn't allow that since that judge was sure to read the law broadly and apply it accurately. In our case that was the Federal Judge's court. I mentioned earlier that this Judge had a reputation as a fair and compassionate judge. His rulings concerning the plights of immigrants who were in danger of being deported showed he had a liberal view of governmental bullying. He seemed to come down on the side of justice for all, with a broad interpretation of the law when there was a gray area that allowed latitude in decisions. I was very happy when I read the order from Philadelphia. I knew we would get a fair hearing from this Judge. I had confidence that we would have a fair trial.

Then I learned that the case had been taken out of that Judge's court and given illegally to another Judge in the District Court. This was the full circle of conspiracy between the Executive Branch, the Judicial Branch and the Legislative Branch. This new judge was to rule against me, simple as that. Only they had to make it look like I was getting my day in court—but in the end they were to get rid of this explosive case and never let it see the light of day. And so it went to this district judge. Down the line I protested to Sydney about this turn of events. "We should protest the change in judges under a direct court order," I insisted. I had a bad feeling about that Judge. I had never met this man, never heard his voice, knew nothing about his record, and would not have recognized him on the street. But just as I recognized the arrogant surgeon as being calloused and an airhead, I felt the same about this judge. Of course I was proven right.

Sydney told me judges were assigned cases at random in Miami. Even the order from Philadelphia was not binding for selection purposes. To ask for a change might hurt our case.

He didn't say it out loud, but I assumed Sydney was hesitant because this was a judge Sydney would bring other cases to. He would need to stay on the good side of any judge who would be ruling on all of his cases, not just on mine. So we were stuck with Judge X.

It came as a surprise when Judge X. ordered us to mediation before he would permit our trial to go forward. In comparison with other cases, we were asking for very little. We were asking the court to award $300,000. Our CPA had set out this figure as the amount of income John would have earned had he lived. Along with that award, we were asking for attorneys' fees.

In those days Sydney talked confidently about our winning the case. He had won such cases before. Depositions revealed that the asbestos used in the Biscayne Annex was the identical asbestos found in John's lungs, coming from a specific mine in Canada proving that it was the asbestos installed by the government and manufacturers that had caused John's lung cancer twenty-three years later. He had been put in a lethal environment by the negligence of others and forced to breathe the deadly fibers. The asbestos was the friable kind that dislodged from the ceiling, walls and floor, and lingered in the air to be breathed. Lung cancer from asbestos was a slow-growing kind, as testified by the medical people. It had caused another worker to lose her lung. At the time of installation, any interested asbestos worker or installer should and could have known the dangers of the stuff by merely asking the Library of Congress and the medical journals for information. The "big company's" claims of ignorance, by her president in his deposition, was the common defense used throughout the industry to try to shun their responsibilities, but it didn't hold water.

I asked Sydney point blank if we were now on our way to trial. He explained that there were one or two issues of a material

167

nature still to be resolved, but he never told me what those issues were. He said we had "a very good chance of winning." I accepted that as a yes. We were going to get our day in court after ten years. I was still troubled by the fact that Judge X. was going to handle the case, but I had to believe Sydney that we were obligated to accept the choice. My own feeling was we were stuck with someone who was not on our side even though the court order was explicit about sending the case back to the original Judge. I took it as a dark omen.

When Sydney informed me about the order for mediation, I accepted it as one more hurdle to jump. All judges ordered mediation in such cases so Judge X. was doing nothing unusual. We were to meet with the attorney for the big company, the representative of their insurance company and the mediator in a neutral atmosphere.

On the morning of the mediation Sydney called. He asked me what I intended to do. He told me they would likely offer $50,000 to settle the case. At that moment, I asked Sydney how our chances in court looked. Were we going to go to trial? What were our chances of winning? With this question I spoke the heart of my concern over accepting or rejecting this settlement offer. It gave Sydney the opportunity to enlighten me about any steps the big company could take to derail the case even if it was only his expert opinion, which is what he was getting paid for. I wanted him to tell me his doubts, if he had any, about winning the case. Most importantly, what could the other side do as their next step if I rejected the settlement? Fifty thousand dollars is a lot of money. Nothing short of losing our day in court would make me accept it and finally have closure. It was a very important decision. I pleaded with Sydney to give me his best advice about any remaining obstacles the big company could throw in our way. I wanted his view of the outcome of the case based on his past experiences and expert advice.

He told me there were only a few more issues to settle in discovery and that we were ready for trial. His best judgment was that we had a very good chance of winning. We were going for a lot more money in the trial than would be offered in this mediation. He seemed very confident we would win. He also gave me the caveat that he could not guarantee a win. I never expected that from him, just his expert opinion about the odds about what the big company could do next.

So you see, it wasn't money that mattered to me. It was public vindication against installers and the government who were reckless and negligent. It was the principal of right versus wrong, of good versus evil. I wanted the verdict to force other reckless and negligent installers and the government to think twice before they ever did such a thing again. An affirming verdict in our case would join the growing body of asbestos law and help others to find justice that would otherwise be denied. My motives were altruistic and pure, but I was a fool in believing I had been told the whole truth.

The mediation went quickly. The arbitrator was a very nice man who kept things moving. The big company's lawyer was abrasive, controlling, intimidating and intractable. He forbade my sons from speaking. He and the insurance representative met in a different room to decide what offers to make. Sydney sat mute even during the intermission.

Sam, John and I talked over the matter during the break. We all agreed we preferred to go to trial based upon what Sydney had told me. Sam and John talked to Sydney too. Again he gave no indication that there were any more obstacles to our going to court. Whether you agree with me or not, I turned down the final offer of $50,000 based solely on Sydney's assurances that we were going to trial.

Sydney had spoken to the opponent's lawyer privately on occasions. That opposing attorney stated, when asked at a later date, had he ever mentioned filing for a Summary Judgment? His answer was he might have mentioned it as lawyers do when they are off the record. In other words, Sydney might have had an inkling at the time of our mediation that the next step the big company could and would most likely take, based upon Sydney's expertise and best guess, would be to derail the trial by filing for a Summary Judgment under the Statute of Repose within the Products Liability Law in the State of Florida. But even if the opposing lawyer did this hinting of such intentions after the mediation was over, it was my feeling that Sydney, in his expertise about asbestos litigation, and the logical steps the opposition had opened to them, should have known and told us that the big company could try this substantial maneuver, even if he wasn't sure they would. If he had told us on the day of mediation that this move might be coming, I would have asked him how he would defend such a request for Summary Judgment. He would have told us what his argument would be. Based on that revelation, we might have accepted the mediation monies.

But Sydney said nothing about this very real possibility. He picked this time to tell us he now had proof the asbestos was the same type in the Annex as was in John's lungs. He made us believe this was startling and positive news that would be the lynch pin of winning the case and he was very confident in this belief.

Based upon that revelation, and in light of no mention by Sydney about the possibility of a request for Summary Judgment that could or could not materialize, I had no reason to think we would be denied a trial before a jury of our peers and get John's day in court.

And so in ignorance I turned down $50,000 in mediation monies and set the stage for a legal disaster.

CHAPTER FOURTEEN
SUMMARY JUDGMENT

In the two weeks following our rejection of the mediation settlement I had no word from Sydney stating when the trial date would be placed on Judge X's docket. My sons and I had a family meeting and retraced all that had happened from beginning to the present. We confessed how tired we were and how eagerly we all wanted closure. The strain was taking its toll on us, mentally and physically. We were having doubts about the trial's outcome. We decided we would make a counter offer to the big company for the amount of $100,000. We would have to pay Sydney his forty percent but the amount left would be enough to make us feel we had reached our goal of making someone pay for John's death. Fatigue had set in. We wanted to get on with our lives.

I called Sydney and told him our wishes. Sydney sounded hesitant about relaying the offer to the big company but he did not tell me why. He hemmed and hawed so much I knew something was wrong.

I waited another two weeks, and when I didn't hear from Sydney, I wrote a letter to Judge X. This last resort action proved how frustrated we were over not hearing from

Sydney or the big company. Counter offers normally were expected in cases of this sort, but our lawyer seemed hesitant to comply with our wishes. Added to that consideration my sons were feeling that Sydney should not get more than twenty-five percent since he wouldn't have to go to trial and he had kept the first $20,000 settlement for that purpose.

Within a very short time Sydney called me. He was calm but I could tell he was furious at me by the nature of the conversation.

"You should not have written to the judge," he said. "It looks like you have no faith in your lawyer."

"I'm sorry, Sydney," I replied. "I didn't want to infer that. I just remember that judges do step in when either side refuses to negotiate and I thought this would prompt him to intervene when I didn't hear from you. Was he very upset?"

Sydney sighed. "He called and wanted to know why I hadn't told you about the big company's motion for a hearing for Summary Judgment. He was angry and said there was no way for him to intervene until that issue was decided."

My breath left my body and that old lump of ice was in my stomach again. "What's a

Summary Judgment?" I asked it in a weak voice.

"Summary Judgment is when all material facts in the case have been stipulated to and the judge determines from a concise overview of the case whether there is a legitimate reason not to send the case to trial. In this case, the big company is using the Products Liability Law and its Statute of Repose to say John has no right to a trial."

My stomach came into my throat.

"This is the first time I'm hearing about this, Sydney," I stammered. "What does this mean to our case?"

"If they win: the case will be over!" He said it bluntly. "There will be no consideration of your counter offer because you will have lost the case."

"My God, Sydney, do we have anything on our side to fight with?"

"The last time this came up, I won the motion. So, we have a good chance."

I felt a little better and could breathe a little easier. But his next statement rocked me.

"I want to withdraw from the case!"

My heart broke into pieces. I cried as I had never cried before. Every bit of anger, rage and sorrow disappeared—I was a broken woman. "Sydney," I choked, "you can't do this at such a late date. I'm sorry I sent the letter to Judge X. I'll send him another letter telling him you had no idea what I was doing. Please reconsider, Sydney. Who would I get at this late date?"

My pleading fell on deaf ears. For many days I suffered mightily. Sydney sent me a letter telling me of his wish to withdraw. Sam called and talked to Sydney. A shouting match ensued. I did what I felt I had to do. I wrote Sydney a letter of apology and implored him to continue. Finally, he said he would. He had every reason to be angry with me for writing to the judge, but when he explained the big company's motion filed for Summary Judgment, I felt we had every reason to be angry with Sydney for not telling us at the mediation that this could be the big company's next step legally.

Had Sydney explained to us that this next step for the big company was an option, and had Sydney told us of his response, I might have felt we could lose the case and feeling that way I believe if that were the case, I would have taken the mediation monies that had been offered. I even asked Sydney to tell the big company we would take the mediation offer, but now it was too late.

I'm not saying Sydney should have been a mind reader, but having been through so many of these cases before, shouldn't he have known that would be the next legal step for the big company? My argument was that Sydney had to know at the time of mediation this would be the big company's next move, based upon his years of experience as an asbestos lawyer. His expert knowledge should have given him an educated guess as to what would happen next, and that Summary Judgment was an option, since he had just told me he had won such a motion in court recently in a case almost identical to mine.

He didn't have to know for certain. He only had to tell us that he suspected this might be their next legal move. We might have accepted the mediation monies. Instead, we were left in the dark with no prior warning. I feel Sydney's silence cost us $50,000.

A doctor is obligated to give patients his best judgment in making medical decisions. So is a lawyer in legal matters—

I still feel I was correct.

Anyway, Sydney stayed with the case.

Here, in essence, was what the big company was proffering in their brief for Summary Judgment:

Under the Products Liability Law of Florida there is a Statute of Repose that says a manufacturer is liable for twelve years, should a defect appear in his product. What they were saying is that their company installed the asbestos in 1952 and the Statute of Repose put a 12-year time limit on their liability for the victim's exposure and injury. Their entire liability would have ended in 1964—twelve years from 1952. In order for John to sue for his lung cancer, he would have had to be exposed in 1964. John, however, was not hired until November of 1965. Therefore he did not come under the twelve-year time limit.

Sydney's response, make no mistake, was a brilliant and correct response grounded in current Florida asbestos law.

His answer said that asbestos cancer is different from injury cited under the Products Liability Law a law created for defective products when the defect could be seen immediately and brought back to the manufacturer for exchange or return of money. As an example, someone buys a doll and the arm falls off. That buyer can immediately return the doll and receive a new one, or their money back because the injury can be seen immediately. In that case, twelve years is a sufficient amount of time. If that buyer does not bring the doll back within those twelve years, the buyer may be lazy, neglectful, or uninterested yet the fault was the buyer's, not the manufacturer's.

Asbestos is a completely different product. It causes a slow-growing cancer and cannot be treated like a doll with a lost arm. If you wish to impose a time limit on asbestos then you must lengthen the time limit from twelve years to forty years, the time physicians' say it takes for the cancer or injury to show itself. It is not the fault of the victim with cancer when the disease takes from 20 to 40 years to manifest itself.

The legislature of the State of Florida recognized this difference and struck down the Statute of Repose provision, but the Supreme Court of Florida had usurped the legislature's powers and reinstated the provision for the benefit of the product manufacturers. That would have been all right if at the same time they provided a new provision for asbestos cancer sufferers that was different and unique. To set a time limit on this slow-growing cancer is unconstitutional. You cannot impose any time limit that bars a citizen from his constitutionally awarded civil right to due process.

Sydney referred to many cases, but the clincher was that the Appellate Court for the State of Florida had upheld this provision that time limits cannot be imposed, since they bar access to the courts which is a constitutional right under due process. That was appellate law that should have taken precedence right there because it was a higher court than the District Court and the District Judge.

The State of Florida had recognized this difference in the case of Owens-Corning vs. Corcoran where the defendant had an accrued cause of action since his cancer was not recognizable through no fault of his own, the very same argument was true of John's case. The important part of the decision was based on the argument that you cannot apply a twelve-year statute of limitation or any time limit at all to asbestos cancer cases because it may not show up for 20 to 40 years. Such a time limit in this case barred access to the courts, and that is not permissible under the Constitution.

It was also not permissible for the Supreme Court of Florida to reinstate the Statute of Repose after the legislature had struck it down, and even less so since no state law can supersede the Constitution. They were remiss in not creating a Products Liability Law expressly for asbestos cases and setting no time limit for asbestos cancer since any time limit would be arbitrary and deny John's civil rights to due process under the Constitution.

Sydney was correct in every way.

Let me tell you how, I think, a liberal Democratic judge and a conservative Republican judge would view this argument.

The liberal judge would have ruled that asbestos cancer is different from a defect in a product you can see immediately. He would have said asbestos does not come under the Products Liability Law and therefore does not come under the twelve-year limit of the Statute of Repose. He would have ruled asbestos has to be treated differently under the law since the injury it produces is slow growing and takes from 20 to 40 years to manifest. Therefore, the time limit of twelve years was unconstitutional. Such a time limit was unconstitutional since it barred access to the courts and stripped John of his due process rights. I think our Miami Federal Judge might have ruled this way.

Now how would a Republican Judge rule? That John was not exposed within the period of twelve years from 1952-1964 under the Statute of Repose. Therefore his ten-year-old case could not be heard by a jury of his peers and a Summary Judgment must be granted.

He would pay no attention to Florida's body of case law about asbestos. He would pay no attention to the appellate court. He would give no credence to asbestos being different from all other products under the liability law, or not being listed under that law. He would give no credence to the medical field and its opinion that asbestos cancer takes a lot longer than twelve years to manifest itself. He would give no credence to the fact that asbestos is a slow-growing cancer, and he would give no credence to the Constitution of the United States which offers due process to its citizens which forbids barring access to the courts by an artificial time limit.

I stand on my constitutional right to free speech to say that the biases of ideology can not be separated from a man's mind. Part of this narrow reading of the law had to be affected by party affiliation, the hope of appointment to a higher position, and a total narrow view of the current law on the books.

Judge X. granted the Summary Judgment to the big company and dismissed John's ten-year case!

This was not the last shock.

Sydney called and informed me he was not taking the appeal. He kept our $20,000 and never went to court.

Out of the whole case we three ended up with $4,000 each while Sydney received near $30,000.

Who would take the appeal?

Now you know why I wanted our Miami Federal Judge to hear the case and why he should have presided over our legal nightmare.

CHAPTER FIFTEEN
THE APPEAL

For several months I brooded over the loss of the case. I couldn't believe a ten-year-old case could be dismissed when the law was so clear. The longer I pondered, the deeper into depression I sank.

I began to blame myself for everything. How arrogant to turn down the mediation monies. How prideful to think persistence would be rewarded. How foolish to send a letter to the judge. And most of all, how naïve I had been for ten years to think justice would be done by a jury of our peers. I saw how power and money can waylay an altruistic cause, how unseen bureaucrats can deny compensation based on unproven testimony, and how the government and installers and hospitals and doctors can literally get away with murder.

Murder did not have to be premeditated and vicious. Only in a court of law does first-degree murder have to be maliciously planned. No, murder can be done by negligence, by cover-up, by incompetence and by ambition. Even now there is no limitation on John's murder if I wanted to file the case again and this time charge the government with out and out murder.

My last chance for vindication was drawing to a close. There was, again, a two-year time limit on filing for an appeal. The prospect of allowing the time to slip away was appalling.

I had no idea what an appeal entailed. The more I thought about it, the more desperate I became not to let everything end when there was still one more venue open to me. I decided to take my case to the appellate court as a <u>Pro</u> <u>Se</u> <u>plaintiff</u>, a Latin term for going to court as a common citizen without any legal training to guide me. Sam's lawyer friend told me they would think I was a kook. I could not have any lawyer's input or guidance. It would require tremendous amounts of reading and research, but the more I thought about it the more I was determined to do it.

A wonderful woman, who was a legal secretary, not a lawyer, helped me with proper forms and mailing procedures. I spent many hours at Nova University's law library researching the Products Liability Laws in Florida and the Statute of Repose. I spent a good deal of time looking up the cases Sydney had used in the Summary Judgment Motion and more outside cases from other jurisdictions that I felt were the same as my own.

All it cost me was a $105 filing fee plus huge amounts of time and effort. I also had to use the proper colored folders required by the appellate process.

It was my understanding that a Summary Judgment could not be granted if material facts in the case were still in dispute. I could have challenged Judge X's assignment to the case and the assignment to circuit court when the order from Pennsylvania ordered it be returned to federal court and the Federal Judge's docket. I could have charged my lawyer with mishandling the case and might have got it reopened. I didn't do either of these things based upon my sense of fair play. I was not going to ruin reputations by making wild accusations that would be impossible to prove, although if Sydney had raised the issue of court assignment we might have prevailed.

What I did was take the Florida law apart piece by piece and offer new facts in my case still unsettled material facts along with reiteration of Florida's body of asbestos law.

First I challenged the applicability of Florida's Products Liability Laws and the Statute of Repose to asbestos cancer. In reading the Products Liability Law I found that asbestos was not mentioned in the groups of products covered. If asbestos was not listed as being covered, then it wasn't.

Therefore the Statute of Repose was invalid for this reason in John's case.

If the justices didn't buy that argument, I would then attack the twelve-year time limit as unconstitutional in asbestos cases where asbestos cancer was too slow growing to have any time limit placed upon it. I raised the constitutional question of access to the courts, of due process, of John's civil rights and of the State Supreme Court's not being able to pass any law that superseded these constitutional issues. The legislature had been wise to abolish the Statute of Repose in asbestos cases. The Supreme Court of Florida, in its haste to reinstate the statute for the manufacturers, were remiss in not creating a separate Product Liability Law or a separate section under the current law for asbestos cancer with no time limit.

If the justices did not buy that argument, then after long and hard research, I would challenge the big company's contention that they were through installing the asbestos in 1952—or that they did not know asbestos was lethal in 1952—and that John had been exposed at a Christmas party in 1964, which would have put him within the Statute of Repose. To do this I had to go back in the archives of *The Miami Herald* to find the stories of the dedication of the building in 1953 and the workers still on the premises showing that the 1952 date was a lie. I also contended that the big company could not prove conclusively that they were finished with the installation at any time even in 1953 and that they could have been called back to work in the building the whole year of 1953, which would again put John within the Statute of Repose.

And lastly, I gave the justices a history of asbestos as being similar to Agent Orange as a lethal material with slow-growing cancer. I cited the court case in which the legislature of New York State had struck down the Statute of Repose for Agent Orange and argued the same should have been done in Florida, and was done by the Florida Legislature. The interference of the Florida Supreme Court in reinstating it deprived John of his access to the courts when his slow-growing cancer was discovered. What is equal before the law should be given equal treatment was my argument. It was unconstitutional for the Supreme Court of Florida to have done such a thing and that the appellate court (the justices' own body of law) had agreed in the latest Florida case.

I also included all of Sydney's arguments before Judge X., noting this was a ten-year case that still had material facts in dispute, and that judges always ruled in such cases that neccessary decisions should be decided by juries and not judges. I pointed out that none of the other asbestos companies used the Statute of Repose to hide behind. They all paid their settlements without having to resort to directives by juries. I verified with documentation all my points of law.

The big company responded with their argument for Summary Judgment and called me a liar when I contended John had been exposed at a Christmas party at Biscayne Annex in 1964. This was new evidence that Sydney had not raised, though I told him about it long before the Summary Judgment hearing.

The appellate court's decision was this: it said every point I brought up was of factual contention, however my attorney (and myself through my attorney) should have made these points in the lower court. They upheld Judge X's decision since he had ruled without these disputed material facts being raised by Sydney.

This says to me Sydney did not do the research I did to discover these opposing material facts and stipulated to facts he shouldn't have. He should not have stipulated to the fact that the big company was finished installing the asbestos in 1952. Had he contacted *The Herald* he would have gotten the same articles I had showing they were still in the building in 1953 and could not prove when they had finished. He could also have contacted the Library of Congress and found the very same articles I had to dispute their claim that they didn't know in 1952 that asbestos was lethal. He could have challenged the Statute of Repose as unconstitutional. He could have challenged the Supreme Court of Florida in reinstating the Statute of Repose as contrary to the Constitution's provisions of due process and civil rights. He could have challenged the Product Liability law for not including asbestos, and therefore not coming under the Statute of Repose. He could have cited the New York legislature, which had struck down the Statute of Repose as blocking access to the courts, and he could have cited John's exposure to asbestos in the Biscayne Annex as happening in 1964. Had he done any of this in the lower courts, the appellate court could have considered it. But, because none of these issues was raised in the lower court, their hands were tied.

If he raised one constitutional issue the case would have been taken out of the Circuit Court and put in to Federal court where it belonged.

I could have exhausted the state courts by going on to the Supreme Court and then into federal court but I knew this case would kill me just as it had killed John. I could not take one more disappointment. There comes a time when persistence turns into obsession and such obsession can destroy your body as well as your mind.

There also comes a time, after fourteen years of fighting, when you have to put it in God's hands, acknowledge that perhaps God does not want you to win, and cultivate peace by realizing you did all you could do. Now it was time to let go.

And that's what I did. I just let it all go.

CHAPTER SIXTEEN
NO MAN IS AN ISLAND

Now that you know the extent of the tragedy the Zocco family has suffered, you may say this book was written with vengeance and retaliation as its aim. It's true I have been strident about and critical of the events and people involved. However, I did so that you might experience the sense of loss, frustration and helplessness we felt when confronted with each setback.

I wanted to show that negligence arises in any occupation and that the people who perpetrate it are not thinking about how their negligence will affect other people. They are only interested in keeping in line with faceless entities like the government, hospitals, doctors, court, Congress, insurance companies, unions and installers who pay their salaries or give them positions to satisfy an ambitious need for power and money. They do it mindlessly with their focus on themselves, rather than on the effect their actions will have on a victim somewhere down the line. I have made these observations in the most hostile terms to show the comparison between the sad things that were done to us, and what we learned about ourselves from our fourteen-year odyssey that became redemptive in nature.

Why did I write this book? The answers are many and varied.

First, I wrote it as a journal of memory dedicated to John. I wanted people to know that he was a living, breathing person with people who loved him and who suffer everyday that he is dead. I wanted to resurrect him from his ignominious death and show the world there are faces and lives behind death and its aftermath. John might have lived a long and happy life if not for the interference of his fellowman that he trusted and loved.

They had no right to kill him in the prime of his life and then ignore him as though their stupidity and ignorance was not at the core of his death. We live in a world where responsibility and accountability are dirty words, to be avoided at all costs. If you can remain faceless and anonymous then your mistakes will never be discovered and you can live with your sleazy little secrets locked away from public scrutiny. I didn't want that to be an out for John's killers.

John had the right to expect the building he worked in to be safe and the government he loved to be his protector, not his executioner.

Take a lesson from this story. You can no longer expect safety when it is connected to others who are supposed to be looking out for you but are not doing their jobs. Just take note of the airplane crashes of late due to government negligence and delayed maintenance. Look at 9/11 and wonder.

People die and nobody cares, except the family. Life is cheap. There is such an overflow of people on the planet, one more dying, more or less, is little noted. We are desensitized to death; we are hardened to suffering; we are glad it happens to others because life is expendable and not in the least bit precious, except our own lives.

So the first reason for the book is to give John humanity in an uncaring world. Some people who read this book just won't get it. They will say, "So what? Everybody dies. The guy is just one of many with sad stories to tell." If that is your argument, remember what John Donne said: "Any man's death diminishes us all, and no man is an island." If we cannot depend on others to have feelings and to care about another man's plight we have descended to our primitive state of every man for himself. Anarchy cannot be far behind.

The next reason is to let people know they must ask questions and be curious about what they are getting into when their safety depends on others. Don't leave things to fate. Be smart. Read about the things that are happening and don't think others can be depended on to tell you the truth. Don't go blindly forward like sheep without checking safety records, taking note of dangerous statistics, or things that are being reported in the newspapers. Be suspicious. It's a terrible way to live, but we live in dangerous times.

Don't be gullible and believe your politicians' or the government's pronouncements. Check out your doctors and hospitals. Find out exactly why they are carrying out certain procedures. Hire a lawyer when dealing with a government agency like the WCO before you ever file claim papers. Find out what your rights are under your union membership. Check to find out the politics of everyone involved. You have the right to protest when your lawyer does something you do not agree with. Stop being so shy. Stop being so trustful.

Thirdly, understand that a just cause does not insure justice. Know in your heart that a cause can become an obsession and that closure is the only way to acceptance. Fourteen years is too long to fight over any wrong. Put it into your head that if you are out for money then your cause is not just and your motives are impure. Money has never yet compensated for deep grief and never will. Remember, your adversaries do not care that they killed someone. If you think they will admit their mistakes or apologize for their indefensible conduct you are mistaken. These people are the same in their anti-social personalities and in their lack of remorse or feelings. Do not be naïve. No one is going to admit anything. Unless you have incontrovertible evidence supporting your case, you are going to lose. Keep every scrap of paper involved in your problem.

Also, remember, a jury trial is always preferable to a judge deciding anything. Judges have biases like any human being so don't stand in awe of them. They use your timidness to make judgments that are incorrect. Here again, in a court of law, pity and compassion don't exist. If you don't have an airtight case, the judges will come down on the side of biases. The same is true of doctors. Don't let their messianic attitudes deter you from asking questions and keeping all records and documentation that you may need later.

But most important of all, the reasons for writing this book are the spiritual lessons it has taught my family and me. In the loss of a loved one under horrendous circumstances there is no closure unless you make peace with your God. The last fourteen years have culminated in a stronger faith and in an understanding of God's word.

The first spiritual lesson is to learn to forgive and to know that all decision and outcomes are in God's hands. No matter how hard you fight, if you don't have God's blessing then your energies will be wasted in futile actions and your soul will be taken over by hatred. God has a plan for every single life. He brooks no deviation from that plan. Your destiny and future were decreed long before you took substance. If His guidance does not include your earthly need for worldly justice, then you must accept the justice He wishes you to have. Though you strain and argue and fight against His wisdom, in the end you must bow to His majestic and all-knowing solution. When you stop struggling against God's desires, they become your own.

In no way does God want you to be bitter or filled with the poison of hate. That is Satan's desire, not God's. If John was killed unfairly it was within God's knowledge. The ultimate result of that torturous fact may be the salvation of others through John's example.

God works for our good. Under that tenent of faith I have to believe there was purpose and triumph in my husband's passing. Even though the world does not take note of, or remember, a tragedy in their midst, God's revealed concern is for the fallen sparrow, the least of the world's beings. John is a fallen sparrow and God's love has noted his fall from life and his death. We still struggle to understand that it is better to be a baby, and live just one day on earth, returning immediately to God's presence, than it is to live a lifetime on earth amongst sinners and be separated from the physical presence of God and his love for our soul. So in that respect, John is with his God and much better off than I am here on earth, away from that ultimate desired destination. I should not be grieving at our parting. In truth, I envy him. My grief is over the fact that God did not see fit to let me accompany John.

There are many ways for God to give you closure. His protection tells you no matter how horrendous life treats you, your soul remains untouched by its manhandling. Closure may come with the sound of falling water or with a warm wind on your cheek, or in a Bible passage of God's healing words. I have found such peace in St. Paul's admonition that I may be bloodied, but I am not destroyed. I have fought the good fight. I have stayed the course. I have finished the race. Those who killed John will never know such peace. God does not let you struggle alone or forever. There is a time when you are free to get on with life. Even after fourteen years, there are more years ahead of you that need living and performance. Even persistence must bow to the inevitability of God's release. Things come to fruition in God's own time, adversity makes steel, and character is born out of trials.

I am fully convinced that godly people can never be defeated by ungodly people even unto death. An infinite soul can never be corrupted by temporal evils. Even if we had won our day in court and the decision had gone our way, our lives would not have changed one iota. It might have been a lift to our worldly egos, but it would have done nothing to make us better people or set our lives on a different course from what God had decreed. Such victory would not have been noted or remembered. It would have been set down in the book of court decisions among a multitude of others, but John's death would have in no way been altered or changed. He would still be dead. But in a book, he lives forever. His story is open to be read time and again by anyone who cares to. The opportunity to know John as a person will always be there. In the end, knowing is better than winning.

It has taken me eight years to learn the craft of writing. I had to start with a creative mind in sole ignorance of the art. In those eight years, while writing other stories and articles, I have honed my skills to come to this book. After this book is finished I can rest. It is the culmination of the work God set out for me to do and it was his sole purpose in driving me to learn and create.

This one book is God's closure for me. He has seen to it that I have never deviated from his intention. His intention was to teach me this lesson, that this testament, far from being an instrument of retribution is kindness to others. We were never meant to win a million dollars because if we were God would have seen we got it. We can do nothing without God. I will never reach his high plane of intellect. He has also taught me that loss is a temporary state that gives in to reunion in God's own time. The world is nothing to run after. It offers nothing of lasting value to the soul the ultimate state of being.

"Vengeance is mine," says the Lord, and "I will never leave you an orphan nor forsake you. Sorrow may come with the night, but joy comes in the morning." (Psalm 36:1)

I believe all these truisms. I know they are correct for the peace that passes all understanding has soothed my heart.

Satisfaction with this book has given me eternal closure. I am calm I am happy I am thrilled with this accomplishment. It is God and John saying there will be a morning.

That conviction is all the closure I need.

THE END

ABOUT THE AUTHOR

LaVerne Zocco was born in Cleveland, Ohio and migrated to Florida in 1961.

Her first published work was a compilation of spiritual essays and poetry entitled *Meet Me in Vermont*.

Her other novels include:

Bara Bey – an adventure-suspense novel set in London and Egypt.

Silvio! – a novella that, though it sounds like the study of the character of a would-be hit man for the Mafia, is actually a study of deep evil and how it can surprise you when you least expect it.

The Friggin' Altos - a comedy and spoof of a Mafia crime family that can't whack anybody.

Mrs. Zocco holds a Masters degree summa cum laude in counseling psychology from Nova University in South Florida. She is licensed as a State Mental Health Counselor. She lives in Pembroke Pines, Florida and has come to writing late but with

a vengeance. Watch for her other books that
will soon be coming to this company.

The Blue Nile
The Hotel Timothy
Palmer Hall
Inside Drug Treatment
Con Amore